# Practising Interdisciplinarity
# in Gender Studies

Veronica Vasterling (coordinator)
Enikő Demény
Clare Hemmings
Ulla Holm
Päivi Korvajärvi
Theodossia-Soula Pavlidou

**RAW
NERVE
BOOKS**

Series title: Travelling Concepts in Feminist Pedagogy: European Perspectives
Series editors: Clare Hemmings and Ann Kaloski-Naylor

## Practising Interdisciplinarity in Gender Studies

copyright © 2006 Raw Nerve Books Limited.

SERIES TITLE: Travelling Concepts in Feminist Pedagogy: European Perspectives
SERIES EDITORS: Clare Hemmings and Ann Kaloski-Naylor
BOOKLET TITLE: Practising Interdisciplinarity in Gender Studies
AUTHORS: Veronica Vasterling (coordinator), Enikő Demény, Clare Hemmings, Ulla Holm, Päivi Korvajärvi, Theodossia-Soula Pavlidou
DESIGN: Hilary Kay Doran; mandela images adapted by Josephine Wilson from Ulla Holm's photographs
PRINTING: York Publishing Services Limited, UK. www.yps-publishing.co.uk
PROOFING: Karen Coulter, Lee Ronald and Liz Sourbut
FINANCIAL SUPPORT: Centre for Women's Studies, University of York, UK www.york.ac.uk/inst/cws
and Athena 2 Advanced Thematic Network in European Women's Studies www.athena2.org
WEB: www.travellingconcepts.net
EMAIL: info@travellingconcepts.net

ISBN: 0-9553586-1-2; 978-0-9553586-1-6

First published in 2006 by
Raw Nerve Books Limited, Centre for Women's Studies, University of York, York YO10 5DD, England
www.rawnervebooks.co.uk

The authors have asserted their moral right to be identified as the authors of this work under the Copyright, Designs and Patents Act, 1988.

British Library Cataloguing-in publication Data.
A catalogue record for this book is available from the British Library.

Enikő, Päivi, Soula, Ulla, and Veronica want to express their warmest thanks to the editors of the four booklets, Ann Kaloski and Clare Hemmings, for their enthusiasm and support throughout this project of making public our in-group experience with interdisciplinarity. Special thanks goes to Clare for her fantastic and most effective way of coordinating the Travelling Concepts Working Group of ATHENA 2.

# Series Preface

*Travelling Concepts in Feminist Pedagogy: European Perspectives is one of the projects currently taking place under the umbrella of Athena, which is a Socrates Thematic Network Project bringing together over 100 Women's and Gender Studies programmes, institutes and documentation centres across Europe. www.athena2.org*

The twenty-four partners working within *Travelling Concepts* have come together in the shared desire to track the movement of key feminist ideas across the geographical, political and cultural complexity that is contemporary Europe.

The partners in *Travelling Concepts* come from fourteen different European countries, and are housed within a range of disciplines or interdisciplinary contexts. Some of us work within Gender or Women's Studies departments, centres or institutes, while others negotiate the specific challenges of feminist research and pedagogy from within 'home' disciplines. Some of us work centrally within academic inquiry, while others straddle academic and activist interests, or teach within a broader educational field, such as adult education. These differing contexts invariably produce different intellectual and political agendas within the group, yet there are a number of points of commonality that we have been able to identify, and the differences have also been productive arenas of inquiry in their own right.

Intellectually and politically, thinking about travelling concepts in feminist pedagogy means foregrounding questions of exclusion, power and silence, among us and in Europe more generally. This work has to attend not only to racism and heterosexism as well as sexism, but also to the specificities of whose movements are constrained and curtailed, whose left more open. Within the work of *Travelling Concepts* West/East barriers proved difficult to overcome, as did presumptions based on generational differences, and silences around whiteness. We have been concerned to make sure that the work we produce reflects directly on these issues and is an invested, politically and intellectually charged map of conceptual travel, one in which we are all staked and located.

One of the ways we hope to develop broader dialogue is through this book series. Each of the four publications addresses a cluster of key concepts and each has been written by a different group of feminist academics from different European countries and disciplinary backgrounds. We look forward to further discussion and invite you to our participatory web site: www.travellingconcepts.net

Books

ReSisters in Conversation: Representation Responsibility Complexity Pedagogy
Giovanna Covi (coordinator), Joan Anim-Addo, Liana Borghi, Luz Gómez García, Sara Goodman, Sabine Grenz, Mina Karavanta.
ISBN: 0-9553586-0-4; 978-0-9553586-0-9

Practising Interdisciplinarity in Gender Studies
Veronica Vasterling (coordinator), Enikő Demény, Clare Hemmings, Ulla Holm, Päivi Korvajärvi, Theodossia-Soula Pavlidou,
ISBN: 0-9553586-1-2; 978-0-9553586-1-6

Common Passion, Different Voices: Reflections on Citizenship and Intersubjectivity
Eva Skærbæk (coordinator), Dasa Duhaček, Elena Pulcini, Melita Richter.
ISBN: 0-9553586-2-0; 978-0-9553586-2-3

Teaching Subjects In Between: Feminist Politics, Disciplines, Generations
Therese Garstenauer (coordinator), Josefina Bueno Alonso, Silvia Caporale Bizzini, Biljana Kašić, Iris van der Tuin.
ISBN: 0-9553586-3-9; 978-0-9553586-3-0

Details of all four books are available on www.rawnervebooks.co.uk
Books can be ordered direct from Raw Nerve or from good bookshops.

# Contents

# PREFACE: Interdisciplinary Praxis

This booklet is the collaborative effort of the group *Practising Interdisciplinarity*, which was formed as part of the *Travelling Concepts in Feminist Pedagogy* branch of Athena 2 (www.travellingconcepts. net). Travelling Concepts as a whole is dedicated to mapping and interrogating movements of key concepts in feminist theory within and across Europe. We are interested in imagining a shared vocabulary that does not reduce the complexity of the field as a whole, and that can account for and challenge silence and exclusion within the frameworks and practices of European feminist studies. Partners within the project of Travelling Concepts have been interested in the effects of translating terms and practices across differences of time, space and language, with a particular emphasis on the limits of this nevertheless resonant desire for 'a common project'.

With this framing purpose in mind, our group decided to focus on *interdisciplinarity*, since this has been a key concept in feminist studies from its inception, and is of relevance across the majority of European institutionalised contexts. There are several reasons for this shared interest in and problematising of interdisciplinarity, some aspects of which will be familiar to readers already participating in feminist studies. As Sabine Hark notes: 'Interdisciplinarity is ... one of the founding and key defining elements of feminist knowledge projects – it can probably be found in virtually every mission statement or program description of any Women's Studies program anywhere in the world' (2005: 10). Yet despite the fact that interdisciplinarity is frequently viewed as an unquestioned good within gender and feminist circles (Maynard and Purvis, 1994; Bostic, 1998; DeVault, 1999), we were not clear about what exactly the concept means or what practices it indicates we should engage with. In fact, we began our work as a group from the shared experience of disappointment that a claim of interdisciplinarity in feminist teaching or research often turns out to be a misleading description of what might be more accurately termed *multidisciplinarity.* This 'misnaming' is an issue we come back to at different points in this piece. In addition, and perhaps most problematically, the term 'interdisciplinarity' can sometimes be invoked as a rhetorical ploy obscuring the problems of hastily made connections or inadequately explored discipline-specific histories of terms. The contemporary example of *performativity* has been very helpful for us in thinking this issue through, since it is clearly a key interdisciplinary term central to contemporary women's, gender and feminist studies, but rarely one that is located in an interdisciplinary context, through, for example, tracing the productive interaction of linguistic theory, political critique and cultural analysis. Without this attention, *performativity* becomes reified as an interdisciplinary term *tout court* and underlying exclusions of particular disciplinary histories remain obscured.

Our interest in interdisciplinarity reflects our deep concern with theory and praxis, and is motivated by both the frustrating ubiquity and vagueness of the *concept* of interdisciplinarity and a consistent lack of commitment on the part of institutions to support the *praxis* of interdisciplinarity. Yet, whatever the persistent problems – conceptual, institutional, practical and otherwise – we have not abandoned our conviction that feminist studies might gain an enormous amount by attention to the practice of interdisciplinarity. It continues to be our belief that interdisciplinarity is one road to (self-)critical and innovative research and teaching, but what interdisciplinarity means should not be assumed to be self-evident. We decided as a group that our focus would be to explore how our working practices (research and teaching) would alter if we took interdisciplinarity as our central concern, as the object of inquiry and goal of feminist research and teaching, rather than as a presumed good or self-evident feature of women's and gender studies. In particular, we were interested in thinking through how interdisciplinarity might work across the geographical, institutional and generational differences that are formative of the group. These primary aims have remained consistent throughout the process, whatever the successes and failures of this collaborative project in other respects.

One of our original aims was to co-author an interdisciplinary syllabus in European women's and gender studies for introductory

Masters-level students, as a kind of 'experiment in feminist interdisciplinarity'. While in the end we decided to set this goal further in the future, the collaborative process leading to this point has shed considerable light on key questions of process and co-operation in creating interdisciplinary work, both for teaching and research. It is in that spirit that we share our findings and reflections with you here in this booklet, and invite you to engage with us in taking forward this 'experiment'.

# Our Story

Who is this 'we' that decided to form *Practising Interdisciplinarity*? The group has six members: Enikő Demény (Babes-Bolyai University, Romania), Clare Hemmings (London School of Economics, United Kingdom), Ulla Holm (Göteborg University, Sweden), Päivi Korvajärvi (University of Tampere, Finland), Theodossia-Soula Pavlidou (Aristotle University of Thessaloniki, Greece) and Veronica Vasterling (Radboud University, The Netherlands). We are not only geographically and geopolitically differently situated, but also institutionally, disciplinarily and professionally. Social sciences, linguistics, philosophy, literary theory and psychology, mixed with feminist studies to a greater or lesser degree, as well as gender and women's studies as an independent field, are represented in our group. Our institutional contexts vary from inter- or multidisciplinary women's or gender studies institutes with an international student body to discipline-based, ethnically and culturally homogenous departments or something in between or both. Our professional histories, experiences, concerns and expertise vary in many ways but age is probably an important factor. We entered the academy at different ages and at different institutional moments, that is, before, after or in the middle of the institutionalisation of women's and gender studies. Clare, for instance, took both her Masters and PhD degrees in interdisciplinary women's studies and has been working in interdisciplinary gender and feminist studies since the beginning of her academic career. Veronica entered the field of women's, gender and feminist studies after a ten-year career as a philosopher, despite the fact that the institutionalisation of women's studies in The Netherlands was already well under way when she was a student in the 1980s. Ulla, on the other hand, was involved in the emerging field of women's studies well before she took her PhD in philosophy at the age of forty-nine.

We mention these different geographical and institutional locations, not only as background context, but also as the starting point for what it means to work together on interdisciplinarity given these profound differences. Not surprisingly, it took us a while to learn to talk with one another and establish some common ground. And although we soon fell into a productive rhythm of several meetings per year our co-operation was tested by more or less familiar obstacles: lack of time, lack of funding, language problems, diverse backgrounds and various personal preoccupations. The group process, as we discuss throughout this booklet, has in fact become an important aspect of our collective work. Real consideration of our different locations is essential to beginning and sustaining collective interdisciplinary work, for the simple reason that (inter)disciplinary locations are institutionalised in ways that are geographically, culturally and temporally particular. This is one of the reasons that we decided to focus not simply on 'interdisciplinarity' *per se*, but on interdisciplinarity as practice, as something that is enabled and constrained by the contexts in which we work, and as something that reflects an ongoing need for reflexive attention to our differences and investments.

Because of the difficulties of dealing with interdisciplinarity in the abstract, we decided at our first meeting in Helsinki that to really think through this thorny issue we would need to start with things (concepts, terms, notions, approaches or whatever) that we axiomatically take or intuitively grasp as 'truly' interdisciplinary, like *performativity*, and investigate how they function or are used within our own fields. The concept of gender appeared to be most obviously appropriate for this enterprise, bringing along with it a number of related notions, like *body, sex, sexuality, identity, subject*, and so on. We agreed that our discussion of gender might usefully serve as a starting point for our feminist dialogue on interdisciplinarity, and as a basis for the emergent community of practice committed to collaborative writing and teaching.

Having embarked on this rather grand project, we decided that we would first need to start at the theoretical and disciplinary or field-specific level before moving to the level of implementation. What is the 'added value' of interdisciplinary teaching as compared to what we might be doing in disciplinary courses? Thinking about interdisciplinarity has been, for the most part, a question of methodology, foregrounding questions like how to start, how to progress, how to learn to talk to one another and implement our own perspectives productively. One thing we are now clear on is that the attempt to find one's bearings in the unfamiliar terrain beyond disciplinary territory requires the openness and flexibility of a real exchange. We left Helsinki with a feeling of satisfaction because of the work we had done, only to discover, a couple of months later at our meeting in London, how hard it was to make progress in between meetings. This experience would become increasingly familiar during the course of the project. There is no doubt about it: for a project of this kind to keep going it is an absolute necessity to meet in person regularly, and this in itself raises questions of both funding and institutional and personal flexibility.[1]

In London we established that we needed to start by sharing our own theoretical understandings of the concepts of gender, knowledge and representation,[2] before moving to interdisciplinary teaching directly. We also agreed to establish a minimal common frame of reference by way of the following set of (influential) books and articles: Mieke Bal, *Travelling Concepts in the Humanities*;[3] Gayatri Chakravorty Spivak, 'Can the Subaltern Speak?'; Lorraine Code, 'Feminist Epistemology'; Judith Butler, *Gender Trouble*; and Donna Haraway, '"Situated Knowledges": The Science Question in Feminism and the Privilege of Partial Perspective'. It is, we have to confess, rather typical that we chose to share predominantly US texts. Although, if we take a second look, the situation is more complex than it at first appears. Lorraine Code is Canadian and would no doubt not be at all amused to be subsumed under the US label, Mieke Bal is Dutch but writes mostly in English, and Gayatri Chakravorty Spivak is at least as much Indian as American. Yet, the fact remains that in thinking through the process and production of an interdisciplinary course at Masters level, there was only one European text, Bal's, published only in English, that we considered formative. We take up the issue of what makes a syllabus 'European' later in the booklet.

In contrast to earlier meetings at which we were scrabbling around for space to talk, at our third meeting in Thessaloniki, we finally found the conditions within which to develop collaborative work: a quiet library, perfect for talking luxuriously, without interruption. Though we differed in our specific interpretations of gender as practice, a consensus emerged about understanding and approaching gender (and knowledge) as practice: 'doing' gender rather than having gender as a pre-determined category. This insight is, of course, a starting point only, for it raises the question of how to go from practices to social categories. Moreover, we decided to set ourselves the task of writing a syllabus for the 'ideal' interdisciplinary course, making use of the position and gender/knowledge papers each of us had written,[4] and with a reflective note on the difficulties and possibilities we encountered in designing such a course. We agreed that it should be an introductory interdisciplinary Masters level course, focusing on gender and knowledge, with the six of us as teachers.

When we met in Barcelona a couple of months later, each with a syllabus in her hands, it was astonishing to see how different the syllabi that we had come up with were. After all the discussions, the common ground we thought we had established, the consensus we had carefully built up, once again, it seemed that we had quite different interpretations or conceptualisations of what we were supposed to be doing. It was fascinating to observe how strongly anchored we remained in our own context, position, and situation – be it disciplinary, cultural or professional. Whereas one course focuses on research methods for PhD students, another course starts with the basics, i.e. the question 'what is gender?' And whereas several syllabi appear to offer a conventional scholarly format (lectures with student participation), some seem to be more experimental. The syllabi also raise provocative issues with respect to interdisciplinary teaching practice. Though our syllabi mostly seem to avoid the boundaries of a disciplinary clustering or ordering of themes and questions, we were each very careful not to overstep the boundaries of the expertise we imagined the others to have. That is, we assigned each other lecture themes derived from what we thought we knew about each other's academic fields. This strategy is, of course, understandable. Yet, in our failure to challenge each other with the assignment of new themes that would have forced us to look in different directions, do different things, than the ones we are used to, we revealed our own reticence about stretching these boundaries.

Discussing the syllabi, the difficult lesson of how to practise interdisciplinarity was brought home to us again. The upshot of this realisation was that it takes more than good will and sincere intentions to build up shared knowledge in a community of practice, and in particular a European community of practice. We resolved to use the summer break before our next meeting in Alicante to conduct informal 'snapshot' overviews of interdisciplinary courses in European MA programmes of gender and women's studies, each within her own geographical region. The purpose of the overviews was to give us an informal sense of 'the state of the art' of interdisciplinary teaching in European gender and women's studies, serving as a starting point for the development of our own project of designing and teaching a European interdisciplinary gender studies course. In addition we decided to write individual critical responses to aspects of the group's progress that we felt raised larger questions about interdisciplinarity, and the overlaps among these have served as the basis of the 'Tackling Interdisciplinarity' section later in the booklet.

# Sample syllabi for Gender and Knowledge: 6 Master's-level, interdisciplinary modules

## I. Gender – A Critical Exploration  (Clare)

### The aim of the course

The course aims to provide a critical, interdisciplinary, international perspective on gender – what it means, where, and for whom. In addition, we emphasise throughout the relationship between gender and 'other' axes of analysis/difference such as sexuality, race, ethnicity, age, and so on. The course aims to break down meanings and practices of gender from a range of angles, and seeks to train students for the following questions: Why is gender important? What does gender mean? What does gender do? In addition, we aim to train students to do the following: identify different gendered meanings in text and context; use gender theory to analyse those texts and contexts; understand the intersectional nature of gender in text and context.

The course will be taught by an interdisciplinary, trans-European team of gender theorists, and will focus on conflicts and transitions in meaning. The first part of the course seeks to address key concepts and theories in and of gender; the second part showcases key debates and arenas where the meaning of gender is unclear or contested. Students will be expected to be fully participatory, and to learn facilitation and presentation skills during the course of the unit.

Assessment is by two coursework assignments, each of 3,000 words, weighted 40% and 60% respectively.

### A. Key Concepts (one week each)

Biology is Destiny I – gender's bodily referent; evolutionary psychology; techno-revolutions (Holm and Vasterling)

Biology is Destiny II – race and sexuality; colonial histories of intersectionality; gender/genre/species (Hemmings and Pavlidou)

Socially Speaking I – gender, kinship and the social; sex/gender distinctions; gender as sign system (Demény and Pavlidou)

Socially Speaking II – performing gender; feminisation (race and sexuality); roles, performativity, subject-formation and resistance (Hemmings and Korvajärvi)

Gender Reproduction I – Gender structures (reproductive labour; horizontal and vertical segregation); childcare; 'family values' (Holm and Korvajärvi)

Bodily Traces I – psychoanalysis and corporeality; sexual difference theory; eros and pathos (Braidotti and Vasterling)

Bodily Traces II – psychic life of power; affect and critical race/sexuality; ontological dimensions of gender (Vasterling and Pavlidou)

Gender Reproduction II – Global flows and values; gendered economics of globalisation; gender, race, nation (external person)
Interdisciplinary problems – all of us

*One Week Break* ──────────────────────────

### B. Key Debates (two weeks each) What are theories useful for?

Resistance and Agency – what is it? What do politics and transformation mean for gender theorists? + case study (maybe historical?)

Genes and Germs – How do gender theorists respond to techno and pharmacological interventions? Case-study on stem cell research and prozac

Gender and Multiculturalism – culture defence, veiling and school – how do we make sense of these tensions? Case study of legal cases

Gender and Rights – sexual rights? public/private divides? State control and autonomy?

Translation and International 'gender perspectives'

## II. PhD Course on Research Methods in Women's/Gender Studies on its Own (Ulla)

— *methodological critical reflection on and utilisation of a plurality of disciplinary research methods for women's/gender studies as an (inter)discipline in the making*

### Problematic

Research methods are often both stumbling blocks and touchstones for interdisciplinarity in general and also for women's/gender studies in particular. Researchers and teachers who have problematised research methods from women's/gender studies practices more often have a background in social sciences than in humanities, even if social scientists are more influenced by humanities in their methodological critique than the other way round. The latter is a general phenomenon. Feminist epistemologies (often philosophical and mostly Anglo-American) have greatly influenced interdisciplinary women's/gender studies, although indirectly, via methodological discussions. Feminist standpoint epistemologies, after a down-turn caused by post-structural critiques, have developed a renewed multicultural vitality.

Newer contributions to methodological discussions within women's/gender studies come today from postcolonial feminist theoretical quarters, where in the recent past they came from LGBTQI or queer-theoretical stances and from (critical) studies on men. In order to tie together such diverse subfields within an inter-, post-, trans- or possibly neo-disciplinary research and educational field some use the term 'intersectionality'. The concept of *intersectionality* (even before the term was used) is arguably one of the driving forces of a dynamic women's/gender studies, since it started to problematise differences. The day women's/gender studies becomes a discipline with rigid methods and a canon of its own it will have lost this dynamic.

The endeavour to keep the field of women's/gender studies open to future insights and knowledge, while at the same time seeking to establish it as a respectable field of knowledge and expertise, has an impact on the question of what research methods to use and how to teach them. There seems to be a consensus that methodological discussions are necessary in women's/gender studies education, but that there are no specific feminist or women's/gender studies research methods. Women's/gender studies are said to be characterised by a multi-method approach.

Methodological discussions undertaken before training in research method skills may, however, leave students confused and without guidance when doing gender studies. This PhD course will heed this paradox or tension between high methodological awareness and uncertainty about which methods to teach and how to teach different methods in a systematic way.

**Form**

The course will be run in two halves. The first half is a seminar series in which one teacher in each session reflects on the possible uses of the methods she has been trained in for different themes within women's/gender studies. Before each session the PhD students are asked to reflect in writing (one page, 2500 characters) and in relation to assigned readings, on what kind of gender studies they think could be done, utilising the methods in question. The second half will be set up as a series of seminars based on synopses of imagined research projects, encouraging the PhD students to combine at least two kinds of research methods (e.g. language analysis with doing gender analysis). The seminars are set up with at least two teachers present at the same time. This last seminar series cannot be established before the synopses are delivered.

The final written assignment is a 6 page imagined project which utilises the previous synopsis and methodological discussions. The paper must clearly state what methods will be used and how these methods are expected to 'do gender studies' with respect to the theme chosen. Each student will present her/his 'project' during 15 minutes at a mini symposium with a commentator for 5 minutes + 10 minutes of discussion for each 'paper'.

**Seminar series I**

### 1. Introduction – an overview of the problematic

Clare Hemmings gives some background to the problematic, i.e. a growing interdisciplinary field, its trans-nationalisation and some of its main but contested methodological discussions.

### 2. Interdisciplinarity and gender studies

Ulla M Holm gives a critical overview of the concept of interdisciplinarity and how it has been used within women's/gender studies. Can we really use more than one set of research methods without being shallow? Can we be consciously creative?

### 3. Doing gender with a social science approach

Päivi Korvajärvi discusses the development of feminist social science methodology and how the 'doing gender' approach can be used in an interdisciplinary fashion.

### 4. The strengths and weaknesses of hermeneutical approaches for gender studies

Veronica Vasterling shows the ways in which a systematic use of hermeneutical/phenomenological methods may enhance social constructivist approaches in women's/gender studies and discusses possible shortcomings of these methods.

Time to deliver a synopsis (7500 character each) for seminar series II

### 5. Utilising linguistic analytical methods for unveiling pre-suppositions on gender

Theodossia-Soula Pavlidou shows how critical thinking in gender studies may profit from linguistic analytical skills. She gives an overview of the kind of skills that may be appropriate for different themes in women's/gender studies.

### 6. Combining different research methods for attending to particulars in cross-national women's/gender studies

Enikő Demény shows how multi-method approaches may be necessary in order to pay attention to particulars in women's/gender studies research that are sensitive to cultural differences.

### Seminar series II

3-6 seminars depending on the number of PhD students (maximum 18) with discussion of three synopses for research projects, with two teachers present, at each session (of 3×45 minutes).

## Final mini symposium

The mini symposium will be three weeks after the last session. All teachers and students are expected to attend. The students make 15 minute presentations of their final written assignments (20,000 characters, delivered one week before). Each paper is commented on by another student for, at most, 5 minutes and discussed for 10 minutes.

## Literature

Assigned by each teacher at a meeting where teachers and students discuss suitable options.

## Some reference material on interdisciplinarity and women's/ gender studies:

Addelson, Kathryn, Pyne (1993b) Knower/Doers and Their Moral Problems, in Linda Alcoff and Elizabeth Potter (eds) *Feminist Epistemologies*. New York: Routledge, 265-294.

Allen, Judith A. and Sally L. Kitch (1998) Disciplined by Disciplines? The Need for an Interdisciplinary Research Mission in Women's Studies. *Feminist Studies* 24 (2), 275–99.

Auslander, Leora (1997) Do Women + Feminist + Men's + Lesbian and Gay + Queer Studies = Gender Studies? *Differences: A Journal of Feminist Cultural Studies* 9 (3), 1–30.

Bowles, Gloria and Renate Duelli-Klein (eds) (1980) *Theories of Women's Studies*. Berkeley: University of California Press.

Boxer, Marilyn J. (1998b) *When Women Ask the Questions: Creating Women's Studies in America*. Baltimore, MD: John Hopkins U.P.

Brown, Wendy (1997) The Impossibility of Women's Studies. *Differences: A Journal of Feminist Cultural Studies*, 9 (3), 79–101.

Collins, Patricia Hill (1991) *Black Feminist Thought: Knowledge, Consciousness, and the Politics of Empowerment*. New York and London: Routledge.

Crenshaw, Kimberley (1991) Mapping the Margins: Intersectionality, Identity Politics, and Violence Against Women of Color. *Stanford Law Review* 43, 1241-1258.

_____ (2003) Traffic at the Crossroads: Multiple Oppressions, in Robin Morgan (ed.) *Sisterhood is Forever: The Women's Anthology for a New Millennium*. New York: Washington Square Press.

Crowley, H. (1999) Women's Studies: Between a rock and a hard place or just another cell in the beehive? *Feminist Review* 61, 131-151.

Friedman, Susan Stanford (1998) (Inter)Disciplinarity and the Question of the Women's Studies PhD. *Feminist Studies* 24(2):301–25.

Haraway, Donna (1992) The Promises of Monsters: A Regenerative Politics for Inappropriate/d Others. Grossberg, Nelson, and Treichler (eds) *Cultural Studies*. New York: Routledge.

Harding, Sandra (ed) (1987) *Feminism and Methodology*. Bloomington: Indiana University Press.

Liinason, Mia and Ulla M Holm (2005a) *Disciplinary Boundaries between the Social Sciences and Humanities: National Report on Sweden*. www.hull.ac.uk/researchintegration.

Naples, Nancy (2003) *Feminism and Method: Ethnography, Discourse, and Activist Research*. New York: Routledge.

Narayan, Uma and Sandra Harding (eds) (2000) *Decentering the Center: Philosophy for a Multicultural, Postcolonial and Feminist World*. Bloomington, Indiana: Indiana U.P.

Pryse, Marjorie (2000) Trans/Feminist Methodology: Bridge to Interdisciplinary Thinking. *NWSA Journal* 12 (2).

Reinharz, Shulamit (1992) *Feminist Methods in Social Research*. New York: Open U.P.

Tanesini, Alessandra (1999) *An Introduction to Feminist Epistemologie*s. Oxford: Blackwell.

Yuval-Davis, N. (1997) Women, Ethnicity and Empowerment: Towards Transversal Politics, in *Gender & Nation*. London: Sage.

### III. Gender and Knowledge  (Päivi)

**The aim of the course**

The overall aim is to further a reflective attitude towards feminist theories, methodologies and ways of doing feminist research. In the course the students learn to reflect on, and understand, the notions that feminist theory and methodology include different angles and perspectives. This fact has consequences for the production of knowledge on gender: different angles and perspectives give different views of material and discursive realities; different theoretical frames have their own limitations and possibilities for the production of knowledge. In addition to this, knowledge is always produced in certain social, intellectual and emotional contexts. Accordingly, knowledge is always local and situated in specific conditions. Research relationships are a crucial condition shaping the concrete content of gender knowledge.

**Participation**

The maximum number of students is 20. The course requires active participation, reading a related article for each session and writing a 10 page essay. The topic and title of the essay will be discussed with the teacher in charge.

**Background: general aspects of feminist knowledge as practice**

1. Gender and knowledge, an introduction to the topic.
    - What does it mean to speak about 'gender and knowledge'?
    - What does it mean to produce knowledge on gender in an interdisciplinary setting?

    Taught by Clare Hemmings

2. Gendered understandings of knowledge production
    - Philosophical roots of knowledge as practice
    - Different understandings of practice in regard to gender
    - Academia as an institution in knowledge production on gender

    Taught by Ulla Holm

3. The challenge of gender dualisms
    - The roots of dualist thinking in regard to gender
    - Is it possible to overcome gender dualisms? Under what conditions yes and under what conditions no?

    Taught by Veronica Vasterling

4. Ethics of knowing gender
    - Questions of feminist ethics

    Taught by Ulla Holm

**Different contexts and intersections of producing knowledge on gender**

5. Thinking gender through intersections
   – Sexualities
   – Ethnicities
   – Nationalities
   Taught by Clare Hemmings

6. Thinking gender through everyday life
   – Processes and practices of doing gender in everyday practices
   – Material, discursive and symbolic practices
   Taught by Päivi Korvajärvi and Theodossia-Soula Pavlidou

7. Thinking gender through social structures
   – How does gender structure social life?
   – How are differences transformed to gender inequalities?
   Taught by Enikő Demény

**Methodological questions**

8. Knowing through the body and emotions
   – How does the body know?
   – Emotions and experiences as knowledge
   Taught by Veronica Vasterling

9. Opportunities and challenges of linguistic analysis of gender
   – What kind of knowledge on gender can be produced through analysing language use?
   – The possibilities of conversation analysis in analysing gender

– The relation of linguistic analysis of gender to ethno-methodological analysis
Taught by Theodossia-Soula Pavlidou

10. Feminist knowing and concrete research processes
– Producing knowledge through research relationships
– Are there feminist methods?
Taught by Päivi Korvajärvi

**Concluding discussion**

11. Producing knowledge in international settings
Concluding debate with Enikő Demény, Clare Hemmings, Veronica Vasterling and the students.

The aim of the debate is to share experiences with students on learning, teaching and communicating gender issues in cross-cultural settings. Each speaker gives an introduction of 10 minutes based on their own experiences. The students prepare questions for each speaker.

**IV. Gender and Knowledge** (Soula)

**Goal** of gender studies: effecting social change through knowledge, empowering through knowledge.

**Aims** of the course: to explicate the role of gender ideologies in the construction of knowledge; to engage in epistemic practices, so that the role of gender/power relations in the production, transmission, and consumption of knowledge becomes evident, making the most indifferent student aware of the gendered dimensions of the world we live in, and the impact of this on the conceptualisation of anything; to develop critical thinking.

**Mode:** the aim of the course is quite theoretical and abstract, but the orientation will be practical, i.e. the course will be 'wrapped' with exercises + films, plays, performances, etc. wherever possible.

1. Start by asking the students '**What is gender?**' + discussion of their (written) answers.

2. Some basics: **gender and sex**

3. **Contextualising gender**
The conceptualisation of 'gender/sex' over time
   – 'Gender' across cultures; emphasis on the norms pertaining to the social meaning of the concept
   – 'Gender' across languages; emphasis on the relativity of designation/designata in different linguistic systems
   – 'Gender' across disciplines; emphasis on the restrictions that different fields of inquiry impose in the way they construct the concept, and how this evolves within the history of each discipline.

4. **Feminist theories of gender**
   – Essentialism: 'bodies that matter'
   – Performativity: 'where have all the bodies gone?'
   – Dichotomies / dualisms / bipolarity / binary thinking
   – Difference-diversity-similarity-equality
   – The interplay of gender with other aspects of identity (class, ethnicity, age, colour, etc.

5. **The contribution of language to the construction of gender**
   – Mechanisms of the linguistic system: the structure of

language, the 'heritage' of informing gender conceptions
- Linguistic/discursive practices: the use of language in interaction, the interactional / mutual (re)producing of genders in communication
- The dialectic of practices and structures (linguistic/discursive, social): practice ↔ habitus ↔ concept ↔ structures

## 6. Feminist epistemologies
- What counts as knowledge? A short history
- Knowledge and power; the role of ideology
- How do feminist theories of knowledge relate to other critical 'theories'?
- Embodied knowledge
- Explicit versus implicit knowledge
- Situated knowledge
- Warrants of objectivity
- Methodologies
- Knowledge(s) as practice(s).

## 7. Changing practices, transforming gender conceptions, making knowledge
- Gender equality policies and knowledge
- Tape and analyse the discourse of the class itself and/or conversations; locate elements of reproduction of the existing gender (more generally: power) order and/or elements of contesting that order.

## V. Gender and Practice (Veronica)

*Course description and format*

Gender is less about being than about doing. In this course we will engage with 'gender and practice' in three ways. There will be six lectures by six different lecturers, six seminars with presentations by students and three workshops focusing on different sets of practices.

The purpose of the lectures is to introduce, clarify and discuss theories, concepts and research pertaining to practice and gender from different (disciplinary) backgrounds and (institutional) settings. In the workshops we will examine the possibilities and difficulties of feminist practices. Professionals from different fields are invited to introduce and conduct experiments, for instance role playing which enable 'hands on' experience of the possibilities and limitations of feminist practices. Both students and lecturers are expected to participate in the workshops. The seminars will be conducted by the students with the lecturers as participating audience. Each student is required to present at least one case of gender(ed) practice, preferably a case reflecting aspects of the student's situation (e.g. disciplinary, cultural, social-economic background). Presentations should include description and critical analysis of the case, references to literature, and a brief research proposal concerning the case. The presentations will be followed by discussion, comments and feedback. Comments and feedback should be reflected upon in the research paper on the case, to be handed in at the end of term.

## Course plan and readings

### Week I    The shift from being to doing

Lecture by Veronica Vasterling
Required reading:
Judith Butler (1988), Performative Acts and Gender Constitution: An Essay in Phenomenology and Feminist Theory.
Veronica Vasterling (2005), The Shift from Being to Doing. Some Reflections on Ontology and Epistemology (based on Silvia Stoller, Veronica Vasterling & Linda Fisher (eds), *Feministische Phänomenologie und Hermeneutik*. Würzburg 2005).

### Week II    The concept of practice

Lecture by Ulla Holm
Required reading:
Ulla Holm (1993), *Mothering and Praxis: a Feminist Philosophical Approach*.

### Week III    Gender and care: How to deal with inequality?

Workshop with professionals from the care sector (a medical doctor, therapist and/or social worker) focusing on problems of inequality. To give care is typically a female practice, to receive care a male prerogative. Compared to other professions care work is not only feminised but underpaid and undervalued.

### Week IV    Gendering practices and practising gender

Lecture by Päivi Korvajärvi.
Required reading:

Sarah Fenstermaker & Candace West (2002), *Doing Gender, Doing Difference.*
Päivi Korvajärvi (2003), 'Doing Gender' – Theoretical and Methodological Considerations.

### Week V   Gender as performance

Lecture by Theodossia-Soula Pavlidou.
Required reading:
Judith Butler (1999), *Gender Trouble.*
Theodossia-Soula Pavlidou (2003), Patterns of participation in classroom interaction: girls' and boys' non-compliance in a Greek high school.

### Week VI   Gender and the Arts: How to deal with stereotypes?

Workshop with professionals from the arts (a movie director, a novelist and/or a museum curator) focusing on the problem of stereotypes and ways of dealing with stereotypes, i.e. ignoring or confronting them, ironic caricature, deconstruction, persiflage etc.

### Week VII   Gender relations, regimes and orders

Lecture by Enikő Demény.
Required reading:
Bob Connell (1987), *Gender and Power.*
Enikő Demény (2003), Open Minds. Opportunities for gender equity in education. A Report on Central and South Eastern Europe and the former Soviet Union.

### Week VIII    Gender, sexuality and race

Lecture by Clare Hemmings
Required reading:
Gayatri Chakravorty Spivak (1988), Can the Subaltern Speak?
Clare Hemmings (2002), *Bisexual Spaces. A Geography of Sexuality and Gender.*

### Week IX    Gender and politics: How to deal with power?

Workshop with professionals working in political institutions (members of the European Parliament, NGO and/or UN organisations) focusing on questions relating to power, e.g. strategies in dealing with 'hard' (economic) and 'soft' (symbolic) power.

### Week X    Three seminars

### Week  XI    Three seminars

### Week XII    Concluding Session: What have we learned?

Reflection and discussion on the workshops and seminars.

# Interdisciplinarity in Geo-Political Perspective

As indicated above, each member of the group conducted a brief overview of available courses, not in an attempt to provide a comprehensive account of interdisciplinary courses in the field, but rather to identify some of the successes and limits of existing interdisciplinary endeavours. Despite institutional differences, a number of common themes relevant to our own critical practices emerged from comparing the regional information available. Rather than presenting our findings on a case-by-case basis, we want to suggest some of the main features of attempted interdisciplinarity at the introductory Masters level by grouping our investigations by extent or degree of institutionalisation of gender and women's studies. This approach allows for an exploration of factors affecting interdisciplinary teaching provision as well as the particular forms and patterns of institutionalisation that individuals might be dealing with. This decision is not intended to reproduce common hierarchies of 'regional development' within women's and gender studies, where autonomous 'interdisciplinary' units are seen as evidence of the fullest institutional achievement (Barazzetti and Leone, 2003: 5-7; Silius, 2002). This kind of developmental history tends to privilege experiences in countries where autonomy has already been (albeit partially) achieved – in the UK, Scandinavia and The Netherlands, for example – which is often more a reflection of the particular national educational framework than it is of levels or standards of feminist teaching and research provision (Hemmings, 2006). What this grouping does allow is parallel rather than hierarchical evaluation, enabling us better to conceptualise what Soula has termed the 'dimensions of variation' across our sites. Indeed, part of what such a grouping enables is a focus on increases and decreases in provision in relation to the particular market and ideological forces we are all contending with.

---

### Methodology Notes

The 'raw material' used as the basis for this overview should not be thought of as representative of other parts of Europe – many areas are not included here – and was not conducted with a view to statistical or generalisable accuracy. The engagements in this section of Practising Interdisciplinarity are very much bound to the existing knowledge base of members of the group. Without those ties, it would have been extremely difficult to get detailed and insightful descriptions from Greece and Hungary, for example, and without someone with a sense of the UK picture, the sheer amount of material would have been overwhelming. Invariably, due to the different

---

patterns of institutionalisation in each region, the range of available material differs dramatically. While in the UK graduate women's or gender studies degrees are well institutionalised, with over thirty-five Masters degree programmes, and hundreds of individual courses or pathways available, in Greece there are currently four postgraduate programmes. In addition, different institutional frameworks mean that Masters programmes are not available, or common, in some regions, while they are a major institutional industry in others. Many programmes are not web-supported, particularly if they run on a shoestring, as many feminist studies concentrations do, and access to sources has therefore had to be negotiated differently in each region, frequently via personal contact rather than public data access. Where national networks are established, as is the case in Finland, access to syllabi and information on existing programmes is much more straightforward, but the volume of available material in the UK and Germany, for example, means that it is harder to give any real flavour of the individual courses or programmes.

Readers will also note that the overviews themselves have been conducted from a variety of differing perspectives, with some providing more background and contextual information, and others taking a more interrogative approach. Our own sense is that these differences also reflect the different contexts we are engaging with. Despite these differences in context and research approaches, there are a number of common threads concerning interdisciplinarity and gender teaching that emerge from this initial research.

## Institutional Contexts of Interdisciplinarity: I

The first cluster of regional contexts we investigated might be characterised as those women's and gender studies environments first established in the late 1970s and early 1980s, with an extensive degree of institutional purchase and visibility typically emerging in the late 1980s. In the UK, women's and gender studies provision is currently in a period of transition. Begun in the 1970s, the field had its strongest growth period in the late 1980s and early 1990s, and currently the field continues to attract healthy numbers of graduate students (mostly from overseas), particularly in the context of joint degrees with development, social policy or media. Yet, while an interested student can take pathways or individual courses in women's or gender issues in almost any university in the country, undergraduate programmes have been wiped out, with all UK BA programmes having closed at the time of writing, and increasing numbers of autonomous centres, departments or institutes having to move into larger departments to survive in any form (Hemmings, 2006). At Masters level, the range of courses and degree-awarding sites is staggering, with twenty-nine institutions offering one or more degrees in women's or gender studies (or variant), and many more offering individual courses. At PhD level, women's studies provision is also very healthy, with PhD student uptake at established institutions such as York, Lancaster and LSE often in the twenties.

Influential factors in respect of the changing fortunes of academic feminist work in the UK include the following:

- The abolition of grants and introduction of fees for undergraduate degrees, which has reduced the number of mature students returning to education, and created a dominant student culture of utilitarianism over idealism (Griffin and Braidotti, 2002: 4; Silius and Tuori, 2003: 17).

- Pervasive understandings of feminism as out of date, which means that students often steer clear of feminist programmes, particularly in light of the need to make your degree 'count' on the open market (Griffin and Hanmer, 2001: 43).

- Lack of recognition of interdisciplinary feminist research by national funding and research assessment bodies, resulting in a disciplinary re-entrenchment.[5] It is within this context that the extent and problems of interdisciplinary Masters provision need to be situated.

Most Masters courses in the UK are one-year full-time and so, in the main, source material emerged from core courses that all students take and that are intended both to introduce and provide advanced reflection for students. These courses aim to do some or all of the following: provide feminist critical tools (a session on sex/gender, for example, is pervasive); a sense of historical continuity and change (often represented by accounts of liberal, radical, socialist, black and postmodern feminisms, often in that order); a sense of debates raised by key issues (e.g. reproductive technology, sexuality, human rights, or education). In addition, depending on what else is taught in the programme, there is often a section broadly about 'knowledge and research practice', focusing on what difference it makes to 'know' from a feminist perspective, and what makes research itself feminist (methodology). Further, almost all of the core courses are team taught, bringing together expertise from within and outside what is usually a small women's and gender studies staff (often of one).

Without exception, each of the core courses looked at for this overview claim to be interdisciplinary, in line with the feminist expectation that we mentioned earlier in this booklet. And in comparison with single disciplinary introductory courses in comparable Masters programmes this is certainly the case. But there are two primary limits to their interdisciplinarity. The first is that despite this claim, core/introductory graduate courses in women's studies and gender studies in the UK are usually more multidisciplinary than they are interdisciplinary. Although team-taught interdisciplinary Masters courses are perceived as the ideal, the reality of the pressures on members of staff in relation to disciplinary research and teaching means that courses are often fragmented and discussion about common aims is minimal. In addition, interdisciplinary approaches tended to reproduce interaction between the humanities and the social sciences over other considerations, again following the disciplinary lines of the individuals concerned.

Where interdisciplinarity was considered to be present, most frequently, theory is privileged over and above other forms of interdisciplinary content, possibly because this offers a relatively straightforward way of moving beyond disciplines. Yet many of the theoretical texts chosen prioritise a deconstructive over e.g. Marxist or radical approaches, meaning that interdisciplinarity can end up being equally as narrow as disciplinarity, but in a different way. One interesting effect of this dominance of theory is that it is often rejected by students on a first reading, particularly those interested in 'grassroots' feminist practice. This emergent common ground seems to confirm (or perhaps has produced) the idea of a theory/practice split that grounds so much inquiry in the field. In a sense, this may indicate that a theory/practice split sometimes occurs not because of progressive institutionalisation of feminist thought, as is commonly suggested in a UK context (Stanley and Wise, 2000; Segal, 2000), but because of the difficulties of an interdisciplinarity whose primary resource is theory of a particular kind.[6]

We did not find an introductory core course where interdisciplinarity was sustained through the course as a whole in the UK; it seemed more present in courses on debates in knowledge and research practice. One reason for this is that these courses are usually taken by more advanced Masters and PhD students. In addition, such courses commonly take interdisciplinarity itself as a separate topic or session, an interesting phenomenon insofar as it allows for the possibility that interdisciplinarity might be partial rather than fully achievable.

Women's and gender studies has developed similarly in The Netherlands, from its inception in the early 1980s, through consolidation in the 1990s, to facing an uncertain future in terms of changes in national infrastructure. Currently, most universities in The Netherlands offer (at least some) women's or gender studies courses across different faculties, but mostly in the humanities and social sciences. Unlike the UK and like Denmark (below), there are only a few Masters programmes in women's and gender studies at Dutch universities. This reflects the fact that the bulk of women's and gender studies teaching and research is integrated into 'traditional', disciplinary programmes and departments, with only a few more or less autonomous centres or institutes for women's and gender studies. Also, it is not possible to major in women's or gender studies in The Netherlands, but there is a great variety of minors, electives, and integrated courses (in various disciplines), both at Bachelors and Masters level. There is a Dutch School for Women's Studies Research (NOV) that offers courses, seminars and other post-graduate training for (international) PhD students in women's and gender studies, but the future of the NOV is uncertain due to changes in the organisation of academic research in The Netherlands.

There are three major centres of women's and gender studies: the Institute for Gender Studies at the Radboud University in Nijmegen, the Women's Studies Centre at the University of Utrecht, and the Centre for Gender and Diversity at the University of Maastricht. The latter focuses mainly on research, while Utrecht and Nijmegen offer an extensive range of courses. Utrecht has recently started two international (i.e. taught in English) Masters programmes, a one year professional Masters (Comparative Women's Studies in Politics and Culture) and a two year research Masters (Gender & Ethnicity). Nijmegen is currently preparing for an international two year research Masters in gender and sexuality studies. Based on a policy of autonomy in research and integration of education, most courses of the Nijmegen Institute for Gender Studies are integrated into disciplinary Bachelors and Masters programmes, covering the wide range of disciplines the Institute's staff represents, i.e. social sciences, humanities, psychology, education, medicine, management, and political science.

In the curricula of the Masters programmes of women's studies at

Utrecht University there are two core courses that are explicitly presented as interdisciplinary. The first is an intensive course in European women's and gender studies from multicultural and interdisciplinary perspectives. Its presumption of interdisciplinarity seems to derive from the fact that the course is multidisciplinary and reflects various educational traditions within Europe. The second is entitled 'Politics of Representation: Gender and Ethnicity in Contemporary Cultural Practice', and includes the 'main themes, theories and methods of Women's Studies in the Humanities' and the 'historical development of intersectional theory'. It is labelled 'interdisciplinary' is because it uses a combination of methods from the humanities and the social sciences.

The Institute for Gender Studies in Nijmegen offers a yearly interdisciplinary course at advanced Bachelors level. Again, it would be more accurate to call this a multidisciplinary course because it has a central theme which is treated from a broad range of more or less disciplinary perspectives, though gender studies is the primary perspective. The course has at least one coordinator who attends all lectures and different teachers for every lecture who sometimes attend lectures by other teachers. Contributing teachers spend on average four hours discussing and preparing for the whole course. Though essentially multidisciplinary, because of the (sometimes intense) collaborative effort over the years the course has some interdisciplinary effects on the staff who have become acquainted with the methods and perspectives of other disciplines and fields.

Though only a few of their core courses are labelled explicitly as interdisciplinary, Utrecht and Nijmegen have rather different reasons for this absence. As in the Nordic countries discussed below, in Utrecht women's studies tends to be taken as an independent discipline that features trans- and interdisciplinary approaches. The Nijmegen reticence reflects an institutional history that has emphasized the integration of gender and women's studies courses in established disciplines. The importance of co-operation for team-taught interdisciplinarity in the Dutch context, however, is a theme that runs through most of the introductory course overviews here.

The third context to highlight in this section is the establishment of gender and women's studies programmes in Scandinavia (see also Finland below). Right from the start there is a problem of comparison, since the university systems and academic traditions differ across the region, and also because of the differing stages of implementation of the Bologna process in each country.[7] But we have included discussion of Denmark, Norway and Sweden here because of their institutionalisation of academic feminism at a relatively early stage. In Denmark, there are few Masters programmes in gender studies. *Gender and welfare – equality and diversity* runs at the Centre for Gender Research at Aalborg University (FREIA) and the Masters in *Gender and Culture* is offered at the Centre for Women's and Gender Studies at Odense University. The small Masters provision means that courses in interdisciplinary women's and gender studies are few in Denmark, and indeed, that there has been a 'brain drain' of feminist professors from Denmark to Sweden. Norway offers two (interdisciplinary) Masters programmes. The first is in *Gender and Development* (taught in English), at the Centre for Women's and Gender Research, University of Bergen, and the second in *Cultural*

*Studies*, where students take one of two specialisations in gender studies, at the Norwegian University of Science and Technology (NTNU) in Trondheim. There are two Bachelors programmes, one in *Gender, Feminism and Gender Equality* at the Centre for Women's Studies and Gender Research, University of Oslo, and one in *Gender Studies* at the Centre for Women's Studies, University of Tromsø.

Sweden offers a large variety of courses in gender or women's studies that claim to be interdisciplinary. Eleven of the largest centres or departments of women's or gender studies offer 30, 60, 90 and 120 ECTS in gender studies, six of them up to 120 ECTS, which constitutes a women's or gender studies major. Södertörn University College and Lund University now also offer full Bachelors programmes where the gender component amounts to 120 ECTS. There is an interesting tension in the description of different levels of the courses at Södertörn. At basic and intermediate levels the provision is described as 'multidisciplinary', at the advanced level it is called 'multifaceted', and at advanced level II there is no specification in the description. On further questioning, Ulla was given the response that all levels are interdisciplinary and employ multiple methods. As appears to be the case in the Netherlands and the UK, most centres for women's or gender studies try to organise their courses thematically, rather than in a multidisciplinary fashion. This holds true for the Centre for Gender Studies at Stockholm University. The Stockholm Centre offers the first full Masters in gender studies in Sweden, comprising 150 ECTS in interdisciplinary gender studies. Stockholm is also interesting in going a step further by integrating separate courses on masculinities, sexualities and queer theory in the regular programme. Göteborg will soon also integrate courses – for several years offered separately – on masculinities and homo/queer into its regular programme.

As many of us have discovered, even when we design our courses to be inter- or transdisciplinary, they are often, due to shortage of time, money and willingness of already burdened teachers, taught in accordance with those teachers' primary disciplinary training. Some centres or departments are more successful than others in creating the synergies necessary for creative cooperative efforts. Of course, some teachers deliberately try to keep gender studies a multidisciplinary teaching field, while others strive to go further. Those sites that now offer PhD provision (Göteborg, Örebro, Linköping, Luleå, Blekinge), or opt for Masters programmes in gender studies, vacillate between seeing gender studies as an 'interdiscipline', or, as a new discipline in its own right, though with problems when it comes to teaching methods and methodology. As indicated in the introduction to the UK provision, above, the prioritisation of theory in interdisciplinary teaching can also function as an indication of its presentation as a discipline as, with a variety of attendant problems in the framing of the field.

Research schools are a recent trend in the Nordic countries, offering courses and scholarships. In the context of PhD education, *The Nordic Research School in Interdisciplinary Gender Studies*[8] strives hard to accomplish inter- and transdisciplinarity. Two of their current courses are: *Intersectionality – Potentials and Challenges*, and *Postmodern Methodologies and Feminist Research: Feminism, Methodology and Change*, with more forthcoming. This school only offers courses, not PhD scholarships, as is the case at the *National Research School in Gender Studies* situated at Umeå University, with partner institutions in

Gävle, Kalmar and Östersund. Their students take their exams within specific disciplines, but are taught gender studies in an interdisciplinary fashion. Here, again, the emphasis is on carving out space for gender studies as a discipline in its own right, which creates difficulties in terms of the teaching of methods and methodology. It may well be that this is why epistemology and methodology courses in the UK have tended to be the primary site of interdisciplinary teaching at Masters level, with varying degrees of success, because of the need to develop specific 'practices of scholarship' rather than concepts *per se*, at this point in the national life of women's and gender studies' provision.

## Institutional Contexts of Interdisciplinarity: II

The second set of contexts we introduce here are women's and gender studies programmes institutionalised in the late 1980s and early 1990s. Loosely speaking, the first set of institutional contexts discussed above might be said to be responding to a range of factors, including the women's movement, increasing numbers of women in higher education as part of a broader expansion, and the modularisation of degree programmes more generally. Programmes established slightly later face similar challenges but, in both cases introduced here, questions of autonomy and integration are clearly formative issues in the consideration of interdisciplinarity.

In Finland, the first separate women's and gender studies institutes or units were established in 1986 (Åbo), 1990 (Tampere) and 1991 (Helsinki). At the time of writing (academic year 2005-06), there were eight professorships in women's and gender studies in eight universities as well as eight institutes, departments, centres or units. There is considerable variation in the administrative approach to organising women's and gender studies in different universities. In regard to their research and teaching profile they differ from each other depending on their administrative context (some are located in social science faculties, some in humanities faculties, and one in the faculty of education), which also determines the profile of the professors in each university. Consequently, attempts to define and implement interdisciplinarity within women's and gender studies rarely take place in a vacuum, but need to be understood in terms of their connections to the specific location and context of each department or centre.

Within this context, national co-operation and information sharing concerning the activities of women's and gender studies is very well developed. There is a peer-reviewed national journal, a national association of women's and gender studies, a national email-list and HILMA, the university network for women's studies, which plays an important role.[9] In short, there is regular co-operation and information flow between the central people in women's and gender studies in the country. This co-operation is a precondition for the promotion of interdisciplinarity within the field in small countries, and its absence is a serious problem, as we will also see below in the Greek context. The status of women's and gender studies as a subject in Finnish universities is still unclear, however. The full implementation of the Bologna process began in autumn 2005, with a view to providing students with three-year BA (180 ECTS) and two-year MA (120

ECTS) provision. Yet students take their MA exams in their major subject, or discipline, in much the same way as they did previously, and it is up to the Ministry of Education to decide which become major subjects in each university. Women's and gender studies are not currently mentioned in the list of major subjects issued by the Ministry, which indicates that a similar form of exclusion to that experienced in the UK context is likely to arise in future.

Accordingly, unlike in Sweden, there is no opportunity to take women's studies or gender studies as a major in the BA exam. It is possible to study women's studies or gender studies as a minor subject (basic and intermediate studies 60 ECTS in eight universities, and advanced studies 60 ECTS in six universities). In addition, four universities provide a two-year MA programme in women's or gender studies (120 ECTS). The same four universities (Helsinki, Åbo, Tampere and Jyväskylä) provide a PhD programme in women's and gender studies. The first PhD degree was completed in autumn 2005. There is a national research school in gender studies in Finland, and furthermore, the universities are partners in the Nordic Research School in Interdisciplinary Gender Studies.

A careful examination of the curricula and teaching programmes of the four MA degrees shows that, somewhat surprisingly and unlike the majority of the other contexts discussed in this overview, yet similar to the Dutch situation, the terms inter, multi- or transdisciplinarity are not widely used, but are implicit in most curricula. However, the reason for this state of affairs differs from the Dutch situation, and more closely resembles that of the Swedish and British, in that women's and gender studies is frequently presented as a discipline in its own right. There seems to be an unspoken agreement that women's and gender studies is in this respect *self-evidently* multi-, inter- or transdisciplinary, and this may be one reason why particular courses reflecting on interdisciplinarity are missing. Such presumptions often result in a 'slip' into multidisciplinarity, though, as we have already seen.

Of course, even though interdisciplinarity is not mentioned, that does not mean that the courses or teaching themselves necessarily lack interdisciplinarity, or interdisciplinary reflection. For example, the course *Feminist Theory* at the University of Tampere consists of seven three-hour lectures given by seven teachers from different universities in Finland, from women's and gender studies or single disciplinary backgrounds. The teachers provide an essential reading list consisting of interdisciplinary texts for the students; the topics of the lectures are thematic – sessions on feminist theory, equality and difference, critical studies on men and masculinities, care, essentialism, constructionism and phenomenology, queer theory, theories of sexuality and the challenge of the body, for example – and as discussed above, this approach is a common one in courses striving for interdisciplinarity. One central issue which remains obscure, as has been identified in other regional contexts, is the extent to which interdisciplinarity might emerge in the teaching itself, either in terms of relations among students, or in terms of teaching dynamics that arise during the course of teaching.

In Germany, women's and gender studies was institutionalised somewhat later than in Scandinavia, the UK and the Netherlands, mostly in the 1990s. While there are many centres that focus on research on women and/or gender, there are relatively few centres that offer courses for students in this area. Thus, there are almost thirty women's or gender studies centres or programmes listed at the central German women online website *frauen info online* (http://www.diemedia.de/f-info/wwwhs.htm), around twenty of which describe themselves as interdisciplinary research centres, or 'competency centres', leaving only a small number offering courses. Of the latter, most present themselves as women's and gender studies centres with an interdisciplinary or transdisciplinary approach (e.g. University of Hannover, University of Arts Berlin, Humboldt University Berlin, Philipps University Marburg).

At Bachelors level, extensive programmes are offered by three universities in Berlin: University of the Arts, Technical University and Humboldt University. There are approximately twenty inter- or transdisciplinary courses out of a total of fifty-six courses taught. Many of these courses have a format that has a genuinely interdisciplinary appeal, rather than simply a multidisciplinary appearance. A certain topic is examined from the perspective of two or more disciplinary fields (i.e. social sciences, humanities, engineering, cultural studies, political sciences, natural sciences), as is common in many other contexts discussed here. What is particular to Berlin, however, is that the emphasis is firmly on the interrelations, intersections and reciprocal influences among the disciplinary fields in question. This mitigates directly against the slide into multidisciplinarity that is common where the critical relationships among disciplinary fields is not the focus. Most of these courses have just one teacher (instead of a team of teachers). It is surprising in one way that a single teacher can maintain an interdisciplinarity commitment of this kind, but in another way it allows for the consistency of focus that is often lost with team teaching.

The situation in Belgium is not dissimilar to that in The Netherlands. Most universities offer some women's or gender studies courses but there is only one full (postgraduate) one-year programme that aims to establish 'an interdisciplinary basis for doing research in the field of women's studies'. The programme is a collaborative effort among the big Flemish universities of Antwerp, Brussels, Gent, and Leuven. The programme appears to have some interdisciplinary aspects. First, all of its courses are topic rather than discipline oriented (e.g. 'Gender and Power', 'Gender and Art', etc.), which increases the odds of interdisciplinary pedagogy being present. Second, there is a compulsory 'feminist theories and methodologies' course that discusses why and how women's studies emerged, what the latter's criticism of mainstream research and science is, and how to design gender-sensitive research etc, with the aim of preparing students for independent gender research. As in the Nordic and British contexts, above, this suggests a development of training towards women's and gender studies in quasi-disciplinarity terms.

## Institutional Contexts of Interdisciplinarity: III

For our purposes, a 'third wave' of institutionalisation of women's and gender studies might be said to emerge from the late 1990s onwards. Again, the issues facing these contexts, and hence the establishment of interdisciplinarity, differ in significant respects from those institutionalised earlier, despite many ongoing similarities. In particular, there are different cultural, political and institutional phenomena, most notably the use of 'gender' as the key for international engagement in the context of development and equality programmes, attending the establishment of these programmes. Thus, in the countries discussed in this section, the distinctive feature of this third phase arises – among other things – from the fact that gender studies has been institutionalised as a direct result of an external economic factor. In the case of Greece this external factor was the EU; in the other South East European countries it was the Soros Foundation. Those concerned with the institutionalisation of women's and gender studies in these contexts need to develop rather different strategies with regard to autonomy and integration than those in the first or second 'waves', and this is important too for those of us in institutional contexts established much earlier, who need to learn the parameters of this new global terrain if we are to survive.

Gender and women's studies courses began to be introduced into the curricula of Hungarian and Romanian universities from the mid to late 1990s, first as separate courses and then, only in the last few years, as graduate programmes offering MA degrees or PhD degrees. We can make a distinction between courses offered at regional level – these are the MA and PhD level courses offered at the Department of Gender Studies of the Central European University (CEU) Budapest – and the locally available courses. Some of the local courses are taught in English and in this way allow the attendance of visiting international students. A number of students from the Central East European and South East European regions attend the courses of the CEU Gender

Department, which has a special importance for the region, when they are funded to return to their home universities to teach gender studies upon graduation. In Hungary the structure of higher education does not include traditionally separate MA programmes. There are five-year-long BA programmes, with minors and majors, and then the next step is a PhD. This structure is going to be changed according to the requirements of the Bologna process. In Romania the situation is different, since their MA programmes were introduced in the mid 1990s, and at present there are a number of MA programmes in gender studies.

After reviewing the gender and women's studies courses offered in these countries the following features might be understood to be pertinent to the discussion at hand. In contrast to the pattern of provision, for example, in the UK, the number of gender courses offered in these countries is expanding year on year, suggesting a period of growth that offers new opportunities for research and teaching. These courses are either offered in the context of autonomous MA programmes in gender studies – for example the Gender Studies Department at CEU, or the Interdisciplinary Group on Gender Studies at Babes-Bolyai University (BBU) Cluj-Napoca (Romania) – or are included in the curricula of MA or BA programmes of 'traditional' disciplines, for example the MA on *Gender and Public Policy* at the Faculty of Political Science, Bucharest University, or in the *Socialization and Gender Studies* programme of the Social & Educational Psychology Department, Eötvös Lóránd University, Budapest. As one might expect, the autonomous programmes in gender studies place considerable emphasis on interdisciplinarity, while those housed within a discipline tend to focus primarily on 'gendering' the particular discipline in question.[10] There is a third form of course provision that needs to be mentioned here: at CEU Gender Studies Department elective courses are grouped within broad disciplinary clusters – social science, humanities and theory/philosophy strands. These might be said to constitute multidisciplinary pathways for students to pursue an interdisciplinary degree but with a particular, probably methodological, specialisation. As in some of the contexts discussed above, methodology and theory here operate to 'redisciplinise' gender studies, but in slightly different ways.

Within the courses claiming interdisciplinary status, above, this is attempted in two main ways. Either courses rely on core texts that themselves claim to be interdisciplinary, or they use the time-honoured feminist method of focusing on a key issue – gender and work, gender and migration, and so on – and evaluate it from different disciplinary perspectives. Neither perspective is particular satisfactory – the first because it raises further questions about what constitutes an interdisciplinary text, and the second because this is likely to protect rather than transform disciplinary boundaries. A further dimension in evaluating interdisciplinary course provision in this region, at this time, is the question of the competing demands of local and global course content. Gender courses at the local level try to build on local research and materials, and to use these to address gender issues of contemporary relevance to the region,[11] but there is also political and market pressure to meet the requirements of international curricula and 'the European dimension' (an issue to which we return later).

The easiest way to approach the successes or failures of inter-disciplinary course provision in Romania and Hungary is to focus on specific examples. The *MA programme in Gender and Culture* at

CEU announces itself as an interdisciplinary course aiming 'at the development of integrative perspectives on gender as an important element constituting social and symbolic order at the local and the global levels'. This aim is pursued by introducing basic approaches and scholarly findings in gender studies across disciplines; combining a focus on the social order, symbolic order, and theory; and supporting students in their critical thinking. In addition, the overall provision seeks to address the demand for an international/ European dimension by including a course on the *History of the Women's Movement*, which includes material on women in the Middle East and India, and through a particular focus on international policy. As suggested in the context of the longer-established Masters programmes, a central feature of the attempt at interdisciplinarity here is the provision of an epistemology course, examining the 'intersection of philosophical, sociological and cultural investigations of knowledge'.

The MA programme on *Gender, Differences and Inequalities* at BBU represents the collaborative effort of the Interdisciplinary Group on Gender Studies, made up of professors from different faculties within the university. This MA programme in gender is currently one of many MAs offered at the Faculty of European Studies, but the aim is ultimately to establish an independent institute for gender studies at BBU, capitalising on what is currently a period of growth in the area. This current Masters programme has been developed 'at the crossroads of different perspectives within social sciences: cultural anthropology, sociology, history, political science, philosophy, visual communication, psychology, law and economics'. Despite this promising framing, the interdisciplinary make-up of the group does not translate into the interdisciplinarity of all the courses offered within the programme as a whole. It is largely only the introductory courses that make this claim, while the 'optional' courses follow the specialisations of the scholars concerned. The introductory course focuses on core texts to introduce a feminist approach to the study of gender; the second part introduces students to the idea that gender is not only a feature of individuals but of the whole of social life, adopting a site-by-site approach. While potentially interdisciplinary, when compared to the Belgian example, above, this approach tends to take sociological, anthropological, historical and political science perspectives as independent and as offering specific methodological tools, and thus again suggests a multi- rather than interdisciplinary integration.

In the Greek context, as in Romania and Hungary, institutionalisation of Masters programmes in women's or gender studies within universities is very recent indeed, and still in its early stages.[12] About five years ago the Greek state began taking steps towards formally establishing some form of women's and gender studies within the university structure as a direct consequence of the EU directive that 10% of the budget for education had to go towards the implementation of measures pertaining to gender and equality. The first move (2002) was a call for postgraduate studies (MA/PhD) programmes on Gender and Equality, which resulted in the first three MA programmes listed below. The second move, a little later, was a call for undergraduate studies on gender and equality, not as autonomous departments but with the aim of improving the existing programmes within other departments. Eight such undergraduate 'cycles' were established at different universities and were intended to run for two full years, in the first instance.[13] An extension of this provision (but without additional funding) was agreed by the Ministry in the winter of 2004/2005, and then, in the summer of 2005, notification of additional financial support was received too. Exactly what this implies nobody knows; but for the programme at the Aristotle University of Thessaloniki, which is the most extensive in Greece,[14] it was decided that the course would run for another two academic years.

Given the situation in Greece, i.e. the scarcity and short history of gender studies, both undergraduate and postgraduate attempts at interdisciplinarity in introductory courses pertaining to gender will be introduced. There are eight undergraduate 'cycles' relating to gender and equality, and over two hundred courses have been offered in the last couple of years. The vast majority of these are offered within a single department and taught by a staff member not usually trained in gender studies per se. As indicated throughout this overview, with the exception of the case of Berlin, in such circumstances the disciplinary background of the individual scholar tends to dominate, particularly when resources (time and money) are scarce. Very few of the courses come close to what our *Practising Interdisciplinarity* group aspires to do, but let us take as an example the course that Soula offered in the last two academic years entitled *Gender Studies and the Humanities*. This course (three hours per week) was obligatory for students attending the undergraduate interdepartmental programme on Gender and Equality at the Aristotle University of Thessaloniki; it was optional for the students of the School of Philology (Classics, Medieval and Modern Greek Philology, Linguistics). The introductory and concluding sessions were taught by Soula, the rest of the sessions by different colleagues representing different disciplines. The course was at best multidisciplinary, and particularly disappointing was the fact that the colleagues participating in the course never attended the others' sessions, or even the introductory ones designed to frame the learning process as a whole. This experience of lack of co-operation is typical, and consistently results in multi- rather than interdisciplinary course provision, whatever the original aims. The pedagogic practice of interdisciplinarity emerges as key to whether or not a particular course turns out to realise its aims, but in contexts like the UK and Sweden the relative lack of value given to teaching over research suggests a move away from interdisciplinarity in practice if not in institutional fantasy.

Four postgraduate programmes in women's studies are currently offered in Greece. The first three were launched in 2003, the last one in 2004. Since there are no departments of women's studies at Greek universities, the newly established MA (and PhD) programmes are carried by different departments; in one case (cf. 1 below), two different departments are co-operating. Interestingly, but not unexpectedly, all of these departments would fall under 'humanities', broadly speaking, echoing Enikő's finding in the Romanian and Hungarian context that interdisciplinarity tends to occur within broader disciplinary 'clusters'. The official titles of these programmes and their localities are as follows:

1. 'Training Teachers and School Psychologists in Education on Gender Equality: Promoting Equality Ideologies in the Educational Process' (Aristotle University of Thessaloniki: School of Education and Philosophy & School of Psychology).

2. 'Women and Genders: Anthropological and Historical Approaches'

(Aegean University at Lesvos: School of Social Anthropology and History).

3. 'Gender and Religion' (National/Kapodistrian University of Athens: School of Theology).

4. 'Gender and New Educational & Working Environments in the Information Society' (Aegean University at Rhodes: School of Pre-School Education and Educational Planning).

In cases 3 and 4, information about the course content and aims has been difficult, sometimes impossible, to get hold of.[15] The anthropological/historical programme (cf. 2 above) does include an obligatory introductory course that comes closest to our enterprise, and is entitled *Anthropological Approaches to Gender*. It comprises four units, each taught by a different person, although, to our knowledge, they are all anthropologists. The three hour sessions address the following topics: the social construction of gender, history of feminist thought and of the feminist movement in Greece and abroad, theories of discourse/sexuality/queer theory, anthropology and sexuality. It is impossible to know to what extent the scholars involved have developed the course together, but their predominant presence in the same school (of Social Anthropology and History) would make this more plausible.[16] In the case of the first programme, it is the introductory, obligatory course *Theoretical and Historical Approaches to Gender in Education* that comes closest to our endeavour, and the same comments as in relation to the second programme pertain.

In addition to the fact that, due to the specific conditions pertaining to gender studies in Greece, there has been scarcely enough time for the development of courses with the same demands as ours, those that do rely on interdepartmental co-operation tend to be multidisciplinary at best. Whatever the intentions of course providers, because of the very rushed (top-down) development of gender studies in the last four to five years, there has been no deepening of understanding of 'interdisciplinarity' and its implications. To move from interdisciplinarity as a fashionable descriptor for courses more accurately described as multidisciplinary, issues of structure and time constraints would need to be more adequately addressed.

The survey we have begun here enables us to situate ourselves in relation to existing interdisciplinary work. It indicates clear areas that we need to focus on in order to ensure that our own work keeps the issue of location and institutionalisation at the forefront of our own course development. To conclude this section we want to highlight some points that we believe are a minimum requirement for real interdisciplinary co-operation within feminist studies. These emerge directly from our initial analysis of the teaching sites in this section, and are all framed by the most important precondition of all, institutional and material support. We develop some of these points, and introduce others, in our discussion 'Tackling Interdisciplinarity', below.

Firstly, where courses are team-taught, interdisciplinarity requires a commitment to attending classes run by experts in a different field. Despite the success of some courses taught by single individuals, we want to preserve the aim of team-taught provision, in order to ensure that the individual's boundaries of knowledge and teaching practices are also extended over time. For such conditions of interdisciplinarity to emerge, there must first be fuller co-operation between individuals and departments involved in (developing) interdisciplinary courses, since high teaching loads and lack of institutional support most frequently mitigate against personal willingness to commit to interdisciplinary development. This fits with our broader conviction that interdisciplinarity requires a fuller understanding of the temporal, geographical and material conditions within which the challenges of interdisciplinarity are negotiated.

In terms of teaching content, we advocate a thematic approach, combined with real attention to overlaps and tensions among the particular disciplinary perspectives brought to bear on those themes. In addition, interdisciplinarity requires a fuller comparison with other terms – i.e. multidisciplinarity, transdisciplinarity, and of course, disciplinarity – in order to mark what distinguishes one from the other in context. On the basis of what we have learned in our initial overview, further investigation of the significance of methodology and epistemology for the development of interdisciplinary approaches within gender and women's studies is clearly warranted, and sustained reflection on the pros and cons of thinking through gender and women's studies as a discipline in its own right. And lastly, interdisciplinarity requires more than a singular effort, but rather a consistent revision and revitalisation of course materials and pedagogic approaches. The regular folding of insights generated from the teaching context coincides with the key feminist aim of transforming the learning context to challenge the de facto hierarchy of students and teachers. Any interdisciplinary feminist teaching project must thus be attentive to student as well as teacher response.

# Tackling Interdisciplinarity

Despite Foucault's influential statement that naming something also defines an identity (Foucault, 1981: 44), in our case naming our undertaking, practice and goal 'interdisciplinary' did not automatically define an 'identity'. To date, considerable feminist effort has been invested in defining, clarifying and reflecting on the nature of interdisciplinarity and its boundaries, and on clarifying the relationship between interdisciplinarity, multidisciplinarity and of course, disciplinarity. Quite recently, for example, Nina Lykke (2004) delineated the concept of interdisciplinarity as transgressing 'borders between disciplinary canons and approaches in a theoretical and methodological bricolage that allows for new synergies to emerge' and is, thus, juxtaposed to the 'additive' approach of 'multidisciplinarity' and to 'transdisciplinarity' which goes 'beyond disciplines and beyond existing canons'. Interdisciplinarity, for most feminist theorists, involves working at the interstices of disciplines, in order to challenge those boundaries as part of extending possible meanings and practices. For Gayatri Spivak (1988), a political science meaning of 'representation' productively overlaps with a literary or media history of the concept, to give rise to new questions for postcolonial feminism concerning dominant and resistant practices. For Spivak, then, interdisciplinarity at its best is an example of ethical feminist work. In this context, multidisciplinarity is in direct contrast to interdisciplinarity, the former bringing together different perspectives, but not in a way that constitutes a spatio-ethical challenge to disciplinary boundaries. From our own discussions, transdisciplinarity might mean going 'beyond existing canons' as Lykke suggests, or creating a new theoretical canon for feminist studies (including interdisciplinary work, of course), although the latter perspective might instead be thought of as proposing feminist studies as a discipline in its own right, an issue we have already raised.

In contrast to the above, we chose *not* to spend time defining right from the beginning what we each understood by this term. Of course, everyone in the group has some idea about what interdisciplinarity signifies. But looking back at the history of women's and gender studies, it seems that the crux of the matter is not so much how 'interdisciplinarity' is to be defined, but under what conditions it can flourish. As Soula has put it (Pavlidou, 2005, 2006a) the following seems to play a pivotal role for materialising interdisciplinarity over desiring it:

1. The development of shared knowledge, common ground, shared background assumptions and presuppositions. This involves more than using the same words when talking about things. It also involves acknowledging the rooting of the meaning of a

word in a specific context, i.e. a bundle of fluid significations and connotations that embrace the word's 'stable', 'core' meaning, as reflected e.g. in a dictionary or lexicon entry. When a concept 'travels' from one field to another, even if the core meaning remains constant, another context with probably a different bundle of significations is activated. To be able to talk across fields in an interdisciplinary mode, it therefore does not suffice that we all read the same texts and develop a common 'glossary'.

2. If we are to create more than just a common glossary, greater commitment and harder work (time investment) are needed because transgressing disciplinary borders involves sustained linguistic and social practices. This is probably the key issue in relationship to interdisciplinarity – but also to the idea of travelling concepts as a whole – namely understanding the practices that lie behind a concept and, in fact, a discipline.

3. In addition to 'understanding' the practices behind or underlying concepts and disciplines, there must also be a possibility of 'doing things' together, that is, becoming a group that moves beyond shared knowledge towards an (academic) community of practice.

4. Finally, it must also be possible to negotiate power relations and thus enable the abrogation, even if only temporarily, of the subject-object distinction in teaching and research. This is important because otherwise we are left with the dominance, not just of an individual, but of one discipline and its 'bundles' and practices, over others.

The point is that neither shared knowledge nor intersubjectivity[17]– both crucial to interdisciplinarity – can in effect be attained, unless they are embedded in enduring communities of practice whose members are willing to negotiate hierarchies of knowledge and power relations. And this insight has serious implications for the practice of feminist teaching and research in overburdened and under-resourced times.

In hindsight, it seems that it is exactly the above conditions that we – productively or unproductively, it remains to be seen – have been trying to enact. Opting for *doing* interdisciplinarity rather than *defining* it, does not automatically move us to a sphere of non-disciplinary thinking: we are aware of the fact that being part of academic traditions that have naturalised categories and borders of scientific endeavour, authoritative meta-narratives on disciplines may still 'discipline' our thoughts in subtle modes. This desire for interdisciplinarity, or recognition of its primary significance in challenging knowledge hierarchies as part of ethical feminist intellectual practice, is thus never quite enough, as we suggest in our discussion below.

Recent fortunes in institutionalisation may have mainstreamed interdisciplinarity, but they have not provided material and conceptual support for its development. These factors make interdisciplinarity as a radical research or pedagogic position difficult to sustain and, perhaps inevitably, feminists within the academy have increasingly suggested 'returns' to disciplinarity as a 'way out' of institutional difficulties germane to the field. Thus, Wendy Brown advocates such a return as a way of countering the reification of 'woman' as women's studies' proper object and ground of its truth (Brown, 1997), and Stevi Jackson endorses a return to the material concerns of sociology as a response to the dominance of 'the cultural turn' in feminist theory and social theory more broadly (Jackson, 2001). This move is one that suggests a series of 'returns' to disciplinary *methodology* in particular. In addition, there is a range of institutional constraints that necessitate such a return. For example, in many countries it is very difficult to gain employment within the academy if you are not established in a classical discipline, a fact that increases in significance in contexts where women's and gender studies programmes are not well established, or whose status within the institution is precarious. Moreover, funding of research is in most cases closely tied to discipline(s) in the traditional sense.

But the problem is that we seem to have internalised such thinking even when those constraints do not apply. Despite the group's avowed focus on interdisciplinarity, the logic of disciplinarity has continued to structure our own practices and discussions as a group, and it has been difficult to move beyond disciplinarity within the development of the syllabus itself. In a way, we took it for granted that we would be able to situate ourselves and our practices within the web of concepts and discourses formed by our various academic and intellectual backgrounds. Yet, in our discussions as a group it was clear that there was an underlying presumption that we each had a different disciplinary background from which we had entered gender or women's studies. And these different disciplinary backgrounds continued to be the basis for our differences of opinion in interdisciplinary syllabus discussions. To give an example: Clare had mentioned at various points that she did not understand herself to have a disciplinary background since she had completed seven years of graduate study in women's studies at the height of its academic insistence on interdisciplinarity.

However, the question kept returning to what she did before that, such that, strangely enough, it felt easier in the end to claim her undergraduate degree in English and Related Literature (the 'related' here being a UK euphemism for commonwealth or '[post]colonial') as her disciplinary origin than to continue, churlishly, to insist that she did not have that kind of home. The irony that Clare highlighted within this discussion was that while this increased our comfort as a group, it was not a reading that would have been shared by her Literature lecturers at the time, most of whom perceived her growing interest in feminist critical perspectives as a disciplinary violence.[18] What is at issue here is not Clare's status as a literary scholar, but our own continued search for each other's disciplinary origins, no matter how absurdly far back we have to reach, as if this authorship were somehow straightforward or 'more correct' than a designation chosen and inhabited in the present.

Despite the fact that we had chosen to 'stand up' for interdisciplinary research and teaching, such issues of (disciplinary) identity and difference kept coming up, and while this may have had something to do with the dynamics of our own group, it also elucidates more general obstacles that litter the road to interdisciplinarity. From an interpersonal perspective, invoking disciplinary differences may be less unsettling than dealing with stark, and possibly incommensurable, differences of opinion (epistemological, methodological and political) that might emerge in discussion of and through interdisciplinarity. A nod to the difference between philosophy and social science perspectives can thus retain those differences as 'of interest' rather than contests over meaning that shape the boundaries between disciplines in the first place. This 'polite' respect for disciplinary boundaries does nevertheless allow our conversation to continue. And the importance of this ability simply *to continue* should not be underestimated in co-operative work of this nature.

One possible answer to these difficult questions is to work towards seeing women's and gender studies itself in strictly disciplinary terms, as is clearly the case in some more institutionalised European contexts. In this vein, Päivi reminded us of the possible empowering effects of disciplinisation for women's and gender studies, one of which is that it defuses presumptions about disciplinarity lying 'elsewhere'. Yet, we were all rather reluctant to see disciplinisation as the final answer to problems of feminist interdisciplinarity. As Enikő insisted, in line with Spivak's argument above, it is the challenges to disciplinary boundaries that mark interdisciplinarity as potentially radical. Endorsing a less closed set of knowledge practices is what gives interdisciplinarity its creative potential. Claiming women's and gender studies as a discipline also leaves unanswered the question of what is so essential about disciplines. Rather than being in possession of some essential truth, might disciplines not be better conceptualised as closed communities of discourse? Trying to attain disciplinary legitimacy for women's and gender studies invariably means trying to establish a common – if contested – curriculum, set of methods and objects of enquiry. This is how disciplines function. But if we work towards creating a discursive community of this kind for women's and gender studies, would we not also need to claim that gender relations should be studied only in this way in order to protect our area of expertise? In this respect, a disciplinisation of gender and women's studies would run the risk of reproducing the kinds of exclusions feminist academic practice has long sought to challenge, that is, exclusions resulting from power imbalances. Instead of trying to gain disciplinary legitimacy for the field, we need to develop strategies for gaining real institutional recognition for interdisciplinary approaches within academia.

## The 'European' Dimension

Being part of ATHENA 2, our project has had to be characterised by some kind of 'European-ness'. Yet despite this, and the fact that we represent Northern, Southern, Eastern and Western Europe between us, we did not initially reflect on what that might mean. To return to this issue here, we want to ask the following questions: Are the European-ness of the syllabi and our own approaches to disciplinarity and interdisciplinarity so well-established that they are self-evident? Is our work *de facto* European?

Our choice of texts to share – those by Bal, Spivak, Haraway and Butler – suggests otherwise. Of course one could argue that a European curriculum should not include only European texts, or that if it did, this would hardly be unproblematic in terms of what is presumed to be European. The hegemonic vacuum, linguistic and otherwise, of European co-operation explains why it is easier to reach agreement over 'external' American titles than over 'internal' European ones. Ulla might know a wonderful Swedish title and Enikő a Romanian one for example, but the frustrating and tough reality we are dealing with is that these titles are absolutely *useless* for pan-European collaborative work unless they are translated into English. We cannot insist enough on this issue of language. Being a native speaker of English or knowing English well as a second language affords immeasurable advantages in the present-day academy, all over the world. At one point in our discussions of Anglo-American dominance in the global feminist academic market, Clare suggested that the term itself made British and US locations parallel in ways that she felt uncomfortable with. And rightly so, because the market and cultural dominance of the US is not shared by the UK, the status of which is more comparable to the other big European countries. Yet, the issue of language dominance does remain one good reason for the continued use of this coupling.

The undeniable American dominance in our choice of texts and composition of syllabi might be a bit misleading here, too, because there is a considerable 'europeanisation' going on, even if it remains beneath the surface. As Veronica has noted, the majority of European researchers and graduate students that she works with 'europeanise' American titles by appropriating and transforming them from the perspective of continental traditions and discussions. This happens for instance with the work of Judith Butler in the German-speaking academy.[19] And as Ulla has suggested, this is also the case in graduate courses in gender, when in a certain country the professor includes among the mainstream English language texts, local texts written in the national languages, or written by somebody from the region or who has written about that region, but eventually translated into English. Indeed, from our discussions, these forms of resistance to and criticism of English language dominance, or American hegemonic influence within gender and women's studies, could be said to constitute a distinctly European feminist perspective. But this European feminist perspective remains too implicit, too un-reflected upon, within our own group as well. Despite the fact that we framed our inquiry through *travelling concepts*, the traces and tracks of the four texts that we took as foundational to our inquiry remained unexplored in the group's own work.[20]

What, then, is European about our project? This simple question has a simple answer, namely that we, as Europeans, bring into the discussion our multi-culturalism, multi-lingualism, our citizenship in a transnational polity, our histories of national states, and our encounters with different aspects of emigration and immigration. In short, we bring all sorts of experiences to these projects that differ from non-European experiences, no matter how diverse.[21] This somewhat tautological answer to the question of 'European-ness' – it is European because we are European – deserves more attention before being brushed aside as *too* simple. For some members of the group this is the first involvement in a Europe-wide project whose European dimensions are well reflected in the composition of the group. Compared to other international contexts we are used to, e.g. Anglo/American and German/Austrian, the Europe-wide co-operation turned out to be more interesting, informative and fruitful than was originally anticipated. From Veronica's perspective, one feature specifically stood out: in contrast to other international projects, there was much more of a power balance in our group. Veronica has theorised this greater power balance as potentially due to the lesser degree of 'language hegemony' (and all that this implies). She has suggested that even though our language of communication was English, all but one of us are not native speakers. Another factor might be that a Europe-wide context is more or less balanced *per se* because none of the European countries – and the educational traditions, cultural and economic capital, linguistic communities that they comprise – is disproportionally large or politically powerful. It does feel more like the differences of relative equals, both in the geo-political and historical sense (sharing for instance certain traditions of education, varying from the Humboldtian Bildung ideal to a tradition of public/state financed education).

The above reflections should not be taken to reinforce the relationship between location and geography within a fantasy of boundaried geo-political integrity that preserves, in the end, a privileged, white 'European-ness'. Yet the question remains of whether an interdisciplinary syllabus can be written from a European perspective without that simply meaning 'European content', which is to say geographically delineated content. In fact, we remain unsure what an interdisciplinary European syllabus would look like, or what it would include. The inability to focus this question is not ours alone – that is why it is pertinent to our discussions. As Clare reported, at a recent seminar in Utrecht on *European Gender Chronologies*, the discussion between Dutch and UK feminist academics continued to make primary reference, albeit critical, to American texts. As suggested throughout this section, is a European feminist interdisciplinarity primarily oppositional, then? And if so, is it to remain mainly a critique of American dominance, which relies so heavily on speaking from the 'European margins', never moving far beyond pointing out that this dominance is detrimental, or the site of power?

We could approach this question from another angle, too. We

have wondered at various points whether remaining in critical rather than productive mode when considering a European feminist interdisciplinary curriculum or practice partly reflects an anxiety about being labelled 'eurocentric'. As Michele Barrett and Mary McIntosh argue in their preface to the recent republication of their article 'Ethnocentrism and Socialist Feminist Theory', the historically appropriate insistence in the 1980s that 'ethnocentrism' was in fact racism by another word has made theorists anxious about exploring other meanings of a specifically 'Eurocentric' feminism.[22] This anxiety has been redoubled by the positioning of 'French Feminist Theory' in an American feminist trajectory as 'essentialist', and by extension in this context also as racist.[23]

Why is attending to these questions so central? One reason already hinted at above would link the issue of 'European-ness' and '(inter)disciplinarity' historiographically. To take 'European-ness' seriously – whether as object or attitude – challenges a trajectory whose lynchpins are predominantly English-language theorists. To think about and through a European interdisciplinarity as potentially more than 'eurocentrism' in teaching and research would be to challenge accepted *histories* of ideas, theories, and disciplines as much as the accepted ideas, theories, and disciplines themselves. While, as suggested, this is difficult to integrate into our syllabus at this stage, what we can say is that it will certainly require more than sensitivity to bibliographical and thematic content, though this is important. It is also significant in terms of how we actually teach the syllabus, since we wish to ensure we do not reproduce a simplified, progressive narrative of sex/gender being displaced by gender performativity or sexual difference theory, and both of these by corporeal feminism or 'new universalism'. European interdisciplinarity needs to look more closely at these histories, to untangle their inclusions and exclusions, and to think through, for example, what it means that 'sexual difference theory' comes to stand for 'French' feminist theory in this trajectory, or 'gender theory' as US, while socialist feminism stands perhaps for the UK – a bizarre opening for national stereotyping if ever there were one. Currently, as our own sharing of key texts indicates, it is difficult to teach a canon while simultaneously disrupting it.

The difficulties of interdisciplinarity, in a way, resemble the difficulties of the political process of European integration. Not only are they both new experiments that receive much rhetorical support and even more very real opposition and obstruction, but also disciplines 'behave' a lot like the nations involved in the EU integration process. Both have traditions, habits, methods and borders that are defended vehemently when criticised or put under pressure from outside. No 'foreigner' is allowed to tamper with them. Tampering is allowed only after a long and cumbersome process of 'naturalisation', but by then the moment and opportunity for interdisciplinarity and integration is gone or, rather, forfeited. In other words, nations and disciplines tend to uphold an either/or logic. Either one belongs, and is therefore allowed and in the position to change traditions, habits, methods and borders, or one doesn't belong and is therefore neither allowed nor in the position to do so. This dynamic, which can be observed within the walls of academia as well as on the platforms of EU meetings, appears to paralyse and suffocate interdisciplinary as well as integrative efforts.

If we define 'European-ness', as we have done interdisciplinarity, not as an identity or location, but as a practice, doing it in a 'European way' – what this means is up for discussion, because it is not something fixed and waiting to be discovered – we would argue that both interdisciplinary practice and European practice should have at least the following two characteristics: be open, rather than fixed; opt for inclusion instead of exclusion. An open and inclusive attitude is a necessary but not sufficient condition for the achievement of productive interdisciplinarity and European integration. National and disciplinary boundaries, habits, methods, and traditions have required centuries of conflict and struggle before they became consolidated as unquestioned values and naturalised as inescapable facts. It is not likely that the 'patriotic pride' invested in them will be relinquished easily. Productive interdisciplinarity and balanced integration requires not only a sustained effort, but also an awareness of the existing boundaries, habits, methods, and traditions. Until we learn to become less defensive about our nations and disciplines – through projects such as these – the numbers of trans- or interdisciplinary cosmopolitans will remain small.

## Becoming a Group

One of the most intriguing and exciting features of the collaborative process of our group concerned variations in the execution of clearly circumscribed assignments, such as the syllabi. We say *intriguing* because the differences increased rather than decreased over time. The use of the word 'differences' does not exactly capture what we want to express here. What we mean is that we do not always use the same register, apply the same conceptual framework, or exist on the same footing. The differences that emerged in the execution of the assignments, therefore, could not always be compared, and, in this sense, were incommensurable. Such differences frequently prevent further co-operation, but in our case, as we suggest throughout this booklet, they were as much a source of inspiration and an *Aha-Erlebnis*, as a challenge to be overcome.

Expanding on this point, as a group we have done rather well with respect to the development of shared knowledge, common ground, and shared background assumptions, as well as negotiation of power relations. We did try seriously to understand each other's intellectual backgrounds and to achieve commonalities that go beyond definitions of terms. Also, we did pretty well in maintaining non-hierarchical relations and consolidating solidarity. While this may have something to do with Veronica's analysis about the non-hegemonic status of the English language in the group, or indeed of European 'integration' more generally, Soula's position was more that this was the result of a specific attitude of openness and flexibility that each of us was determined to bring with us. And yet, despite our good communicative habits, whatever their basis, the simple fact that not all of us could be at all of the meetings together effected a variant degree of access to the group's shared knowledge and, consequently, the distribution of power.

These disparities and their resultant tensions have a direct bearing on our theorisation of feminist interdisciplinarity. First of all, we identified a tension with respect to the degree of one's identification (or coincidence) with the group's work. Some of us, being centrally positioned in women's or gender studies, came into the group with our full academic selves, so to speak. Although this may sound too simplistic, what is meant is that some of us merely had to extend the radius of our activities within the field. For those positioned primarily within a discipline, things looked a bit different. To give just one example, it took Soula a while to admit to herself that the group's work, sacred as it may be, is only one out of five major areas of academic activities that she undertakes, in addition to her 'regular' job in the Linguistics Department. Although she kept hoping to be able to develop a unified attitude or approach to all six areas, she has had to recognise that this has not yet been achieved; so, of her 'fragmented' (though not split) self, only one side could ever really be present within the group.

These kinds of reflections are important for what they reveal about our intellectual presumptions. Soula's analysis provides a rather different take on the disciplinarity/interdisciplinarity discussion we had above, in which interdisciplinarity was framed as subject to habitually dominant *disciplinary* certainties. Here, instead, it might be that it is a 'generational', or institutional, feminist interdisciplinarity that is presumed, and feminist disciplinarity that struggles for visibility, and indeed, is frequently blamed for a somewhat aggressive visibility if successful. It is perhaps indicative of this dynamic that the disadvantages of disciplinary location have not been addressed until this concluding section of the booklet, while the difficulties of being misunderstood as an interdisciplinary scholar have taken centre stage.[24] One might add here, too, that this insight is particularly important for feminist studies, given that the vast majority of its practitioners work within disciplinary contexts at the institutional level.

The second tension has to do with time: how much time each of us could invest in the group's work and the fact that the time for achieving the goals of the group as a whole was never sufficient. Inevitable time constraints result in the difference between intention and reality, probably one of the key features of practising interdisciplinarity. Looking back, our work might be said to have been characterised by spasmodic movements as we sought an ongoing compromise between what we wanted to do and the real conditions under which we had to do it. The fact, however, that the stumbling blocks were encountered within the context of our co-operative effort enabled an important feature of interdisciplinary intention to materialise – when one person was overwhelmed with other responsibilities or constraints, sick, or otherwise unable to focus on the project, someone else was always able to step in. Given the inevitable difficulties of interdisciplinary work, perhaps co-operation is a necessity rather than a hindrance. Certainly, for us, it has been the most exciting feature of our project.

## Looking Forward

Interdisciplinarity starts with the people who practice it. Our group process confirms this view. Throughout our work together we have discovered that interdisciplinarity is inherently a question of conversation, of dialogue and co-operation. Writing this booklet together has been a good training ground for our plans for the future – assembling and teaching together an interdisciplinary course at several European gender and women's studies centres. The Institute for Gender Studies at the Radboud University in Nijmegen and its equivalent at the Humboldt University in Berlin have already expressed an interest in such a 'travelling course'. This will give us the opportunity to reflect on the actual teaching process, on the implications of situatedness and, of course, on some of the real opportunities and limitations of interdisciplinary courses.

## Notes

[1] These issues are themselves fundamentally gendered – women in academia earn consistently less than men in parallel positions, and are more likely to have dependents.

[2] The last of these was subsequently dropped.

[3] As readers will no doubt have noticed, the Travelling Concepts group as a whole has borrowed Mieke Bal's term for our own pedagogic explorations here.

[4] The position papers represent the work of the Travelling Concepts group as a whole, and form the basis of the interactive website 'Travelling Concepts in Feminist Pedagogy', at www.travellingconcepts.net.

[5] This is particularly ironic in the context of women's and gender studies, whose health at the graduate level is largely dependent on overseas students who come to the UK precisely because it offers interdisciplinary research on gender.

[6] In addition one might argue that the development of a common theoretical ground is more akin to the 'disciplinisation' of gender and women's studies.

[7] Though Sweden was among the first countries in the region to have established women's and gender studies programmes, Iceland, Denmark and Norway are ahead of Sweden in implementing Bachelors or Masters programmes.

[8] http://www.tema.liu.se/tema-g/norfa.htm – The Nordic Research School in Interdisciplinary Gender Studies is coordinated in Sweden, with partners from other Nordic countries, Baltic countries and North West Russia.

[9] In teaching, HILMA's most visible activity has been the development of nationwide web-based courses. HILMA has an established board, made up of all the professors and a development group consisting of representatives from each unit of women's and gender studies. Both the board and the development group have two to three meetings each year. In addition, HILMA holds an annual two day seminar. See http://www.helsinki.fi/hilma/en_ja_ru/index_en.htm

[10] This combination approach fits well with a current academic consensus of sorts, that gender and women's studies works most effectively when focused on both autonomy and integration (Bergman, 2000: 52; Stacey, Phoenix and Hinds, 1992: 5; Braidotti, 2002: 288).

[11] Thus in Bulgaria several courses use local materials, and in Sarajevo a course on gender and war takes a similar approach.

[12] Although this should not be taken to imply that gender-relevant courses were not being offered. In some departments they have been available for as long as twenty years.

[13] The experiences gained from these programmes during the first two years were presented at the conference 'Gender Studies in Greece and Abroad: Assessment and Perspectives', taking into account the South East European context and the broader European theoretical discussion. This conference was organised at the Artistotle University of Thessaloniki, Spring 2005 (see Pavlidou, 2006b).

[14] It involves 13 different departments, though some of them are only marginally participating, offering a total of about 50 courses a year.

[15] The lack of communication among departments is of course central to the challenges of interdisciplinary work, since willingness to co-operate is such a key feature of interdisciplinary gender studies provision, as was pointed out in the Finnish context. Yet, departments are frequently pitted one against the other in the quest for scarce resources.

[16] This possibility raises an interesting issue for interdisciplinary gender studies, particularly when read together with the Berlin context Veronica explored, above: that it may be easier to create the environment necessary for interdisciplinary work within a single discipline (or even a single individual) than it is when people are brought in from different environments.

[17] See our colleagues' booklet on intersubjectivity for a fuller elaboration of this concept: Eva Skærbæk, Dasa Duhaček, Elena Pulcini, Melita Richter, *Common Passion, Different Voices: Reflections on Citizenship and Intersubjectivity* (Raw Nerve, 2006).

[18] A typical response to an undergraduate paper using feminist analysis was: 'I will not be bullied by feminism into giving this dreadful paper a better mark than it deserves'. The issue here is not whether the paper was a good one – it was, in fact, quite awful – but that this particular proponent of the discipline identitified feminism itself as both marginal to it and a 'bully'.

[19] See for instance the contributions of Halsema, Stoller and Vasterling in S. Stoller, V. Vasterling and L. Fisher (eds) 2005.

[20] An interesting project that would be indeed: to trace the significance of, for example, Spivak's take-up in European feminist pedagogy, the effects, particularly for her, of translation of her work into contexts sharing much or little of the distinctive contexts and disjunctures that frame the original text.

[21] To be able to delineate our project from not only an American one, but also similar projects in other continents, we would have to define first what typified these other projects. Since this is not the focus of the group, it would be completely outside our reach to do so.

[22] The contemporary South African novelist Achmat Dangor ironically highlights ways in which anything 'taking place in' Europe can be politically dubbed 'eurocentric', through his staging of students' refusal to read Virgil on that basis (2004).

[23] See Hemmings 2005 for an account of the slip between 'essentialism' and 'racism' that works by positioning sexual difference theory as having been effectively critiqued (and dispensed with) by critical race and poststructuralist scholars.

[24] These differences are not just generational of course, but that is certainly one area needing a reflexive engagement to avoid obscuring material power relations that structure our access to participation in collaborative feminist work.

# BIBLIOGRAPHY

Bal, Mieke (2002) *Travelling Concepts in the Humanities: a Rough Guide.* University of Toronto Press.

Barazzetti, Donatella and Mariagrazia Leone (2003) The Institutionalisation of Women's Studies Training in Europe, in *Comparative Data Report 2. Employment and Women's Studies: The Impact of Women's Studies Training of Women's Employment in Europe.* The University of Hull.

Bergman, Solveig (2000) Women's Studies in the Nordic Countries: Organisation,Strategies and Resources, in *The Making of European Women's Studies*, Volume II. Athena/Universiteit Utrecht, 51-66.

Bostic, Joy (1998) It's a Jazz Thang: Interdisciplinarity and Critical Imagining in the Construction of a Womanist Theological Method, in K. Conway-Turner et al.(eds) *Women's Studies in Transition: the Pursuit of Interdisciplinarity.* University of Delaware Press, 138-155.

Braidotti, Rosi (2002)The Uses and Abuses of the Sex/Gender Distinction in European Feminist Practices, in G. Griffin and R. Braidotti (eds), *ThinkingDifferently: A Reader in European Women's Studies.* London: Zed Books, 285-307.

Brown, Wendy (1997) The Impossibility of Women's Studies, in *differences: a Journal of Feminist Cultural Studies* 9 (3), 79-90.

Butler, Judith (1990) *Gender Trouble: Feminism and Subversion of Identity.* New York: Routledge.

Dangor, Achmat (2001) *Bitter Fruit.* Cape Town: Kwela Books.

DeVault, M. L. (1999) Becoming a Feminist Scholar: a Second-Generation Story, in *Liberating Method: Feminism and Social Research*. Philadelphia University Press, 5-19.

Griffin, Gabriele and Rosi Braidotti (2002) Introduction: Configuring European Women's Studies, in G. Griffin and R. Braidotti (eds), *Thinking Differently: A Reader in European Women's Studies*. London: Zed Books, 1-28.

_____ and Jalna Hanmer (2001). Background Data Report: UK, in *Employment and Women's Studies: The Impact of Women's Studies Training on Women's Employment in Europe*. The University of Hull.

Haraway, Donna (1988) 'Situated Knowledges': the Science Question in Feminism and the Privilege of Partial Perspective, in *Feminist Studies* 14 (3), 581-607.

_____ (1990) A Manifesto for Cyborgs: Science, Technology and Socialist Feminism in the 1980s, in *Simians, Cyborgs and Women: the Reinvention of Nature*. London: Free Association Press.

Hark, Sabine (2005) Blurring Boundaries, Crossing Borders, Traversing Frontiers: Inter- and Transdisciplinarity Revisited, Paper at the workshop of the EU funded research project 'Disciplinary Barriers between the Social Sciences and the Humanities', Turku/Abo, Finland, June 9-11.

Hemmings, Clare (2005) Telling Feminist Stories, in *Feminist Theory* 6 (2), 115-139.

_____ (2006) The Life and Times of Academic Feminism, in Kathy Davis, Mary Evans and Judith Lorber (eds) *Handbook of Gender and Women's Studies*. London: Sage, 13-24.

Jackson, Stevi (2001) Why a Materialist Feminism is (Still) Possible and Necessary, in *Women's Studies International Forum* 24 (3-4), 283-293.

Maynard, Mary and June Purvis (eds) (1994) *Researching Women's Lives from a Feminist Perspective.* London: Taylor and Francis.

Pavlidou, Theodossia-Soula (2005) Interdisciplinarity. Presentation at the Conference on 'Travelling Concepts in Feminist Pedagogy' at Humboldt Universität zu Berlin, June 10, 2005.

_____ (2006a) Interdisciplinarity: Queries and Quandaries, in *Travelling Concepts in Feminist Pedagogy: European Perspectives.* York: Raw Nerve, http:www.travellingconcepts.net.

_____ (ed) (2006b) *Gender Studies: Tensions/Trends in Greece and Other European Countries.* Thessaloniki: Zitis.

Segal, Lynne (2000) Only Contradictions on Offer, in *Women: a Cultural Review* 11 (1-2), 19-36.

Silius, Harriet (2002) Women's Employment, Equal Opportunities and Women's Studies in Nine European Countries – a Summary, in *Employment and Women's Studies: The Impact of Women's Studies Training of Women's Employment in Europe.* The University of Hull.

_____ and Salla Tuori (2003) Professionalisation of Women's Studies Graduates (including academic profession) in Europe, in *Comparative Data Report 6. Employment and Women's Studies: The Impact of Women's Studies Training of Women's Employment in Europe.* The University of Hull.

Spivak, Gayatri (1988) Can the Subaltern Speak?, in C. Nelson and L. Grossberg (eds) *Marxism and the Interpretation of Culture.* Houndsmills: Macmillan.

Stanley, Elizabeth and Sue Wise (2000) But the Empress has no Clothes! Some Awkward Questions about 'the Missing Revolution' in Feminist Theory, in *Feminist Theory* 1 (3), 261-288.

Stacey, Jackie, Ann Phoenix and Hilary Hinds (1992) Working Out: New Directions for Women's Studies, in H. Hinds, A. Phoenix and J. Stacey (eds) *Working Out: New Directions for Women's Studies.* London: Palmer Press, 1-10.

Stoller, Silvia, Veronica Vasterling and Linda Fisher (eds) (2005) *Feministische Phänomenologie und Hermeneutik.* Würzburg: Königshausen & Neumann.

Reader's Notes

Reader's Notes

Reader's Notes